Presidential Legislative Activity

Using Quantifiable Measures to Explore Leadership in the American System

Carl D. Cavalli

University Press of America,® Inc.
Dallas · Lanham · Boulder · New York · Oxford

To Alfred and Marie, and to B.J.

Table of Contents

Preface   vii

Acknowledgements   ix

Chapter 1: Presidential Leadership   1

Chapter 2: Power and Influence   5
   Normative Studies of Power   5
   Measures of Influence   7

Chapter 3: Categorizing Legislative Activities   11
   Type of Activity   11
   Dimensions   13
   Amount of Activity   13
   Discussion of Type and Amount   13

Chapter 4: Gathering the Data   15
   Sources of Presidential Activity Data   15
   Coding the Data   21

Chapter 5: Coding the Data — Some Detailed Examples   29
   Typical Coding   29
   Persuasion   33
   Inducement   34
   Organization   39

Emphasis   42

Chapter 6: Considerations of Validity and Reliability   47
Some Initial Notes on the Samples   47

Chapter 7: Results I   61
Organization Over Time   61
Strategy and Legislative Experience   65
Cyclical Effects   69
Legislative Experience and Activity   71
Other Possibilities   75

Chapter 8: Results II   79
Contact Data   79
Contact Data and the Case of Wilbur Mills   79
Contact Data Analysis   80
A Consideration for Future Exploration   94
Summary   95

Chapter 9: Discussion   97
What Has Been Learned?   97
Presidential Leadership in the American System   98
The Bottom Line   100

Chapter 10: 'Quantitative Biography' and the Future   101
Cliometrics   102
Applying Cliometrics to Presidential Studies   103
The Present and Future   104
Some Thoughts About Future Research   105
Some Hypotheses for the Future   109

Bibliography   111

About the Author   121

Index   123

Preface

The idea for this work came from the simple observation of a graduate student pursuing studies of the presidency many years ago. I noticed that for all the speculation and descriptive accounts about presidential activity, there was no systematic accounting of what presidents *do*. As with much of the discipline of political science, studies of the presidency have changed over time from largely historical and biographical explorations to more methodologically rigorous ones. Yet the actual behavior of presidents was still the province of anecdotal description and behind-the-scenes, 'kiss and tell' books. It became clear that academic explorations of the presidency can greatly benefit from the development of a typology of presidential activities. This would allow us to actually see what presidents do. This became the focus of my doctoral dissertation — to develop such a typology, and to use samples from several administrations to explore questions about presidential behavior. The analyses in this project confirm much of the heretofore descriptive and anecdotal evidence on such things as levels of presidential activity and travel, but dispute the popular conception of presidents being legislators first and foremost.

One advantage of using this data is to fight the much-lamented problem of the 'small-N'. This is the notion, common in much presidential literature, that the presidency is not amenable to statistical analysis because there have only been about a dozen 'modern' presidents (from FDR to the present). But with activity data, the 'N' is no longer the president, it is the activity. It changes from too small to analyze to seemingly infinite and amenable to very rich analysis. Activity data allow us to explore commonalities across presidencies, instead of labeling each administration as somehow unique. For example, we will see in this analysis that some support exists for the notion that presidents behave differently in election years than in non-election years. This is not an astounding revelation, but we now have a way to systematically explore these behaviors. Another advantage is the ability to explore empirically the president's relationship with Congress. Finally, this also allows us to explore the substantive parameters of presidential legislative success.

Carl D. Cavalli,
Dahlonega, Georgia,
March 2004

Acknowledgments

I would like to recognize the contributions of the following people and institutions:

My dissertation committee, directed by Terry Sullivan, with readers David Lowery, Michael MacKuen, George Rabinowitz, and James Stimson. Their helpful review and comments made this a better work.

The Dwight D. Eisenhower Library and Museum, The Lyndon Baines Johnson Library and Museum, The Nixon Project of the National Archives, and the helpful staff in each. Part of the task of this work was to promote the value of the data contained in these and other presidential libraries. They confirmed my thoughts.

Portions of this research were funded by a research grant from the Lyndon Baines Johnson Foundation. Thank you.

All of the above made this a better book. Any errors are, of course, my own.

Portions of this material appeared in the Vol. 28, Number 2 (June 2000) issue of the journal *Southeastern Political Review* in the article "Quantitative Biography: A "Cliometric" Approach to Presidential Studies."

Chapter 1: Presidential Leadership

Everybody now expects the man inside the White House to do something about everything. Laws and customs now reflect acceptance of him as the great initiator, an acceptance quite as widespread at the Capitol as at his end of Pennsylvania Avenue.

-Richard Neustadt
Presidential Power

We have come to expect the president to act as policy leader: to set the agenda and to engineer passage of legislation to deal with the country's major problems.

-Barbara Sinclair
"Trying to Govern Positively in a Negative Era: Clinton and the 103rd Congress"

Our expectations of contemporary presidential leadership are always legislative in nature. We choose presidents not for their executive abilities, but rather for their legislative proposals. We judge them not by their ability to implement the laws of the land, but by their ability to get their proposals enacted into law. Several years after the opening quote, Richard Neustadt (1969) again noted that "we have made a matter of routine the president's responsibility to take the policy lead." Recently, the presidential role which Clinton Rossiter (1956) defines as Chief Legislator became the locus of full-blown concepts of the presidency (Wayne 1978; Light 1983; Edwards 1989; Bond and Fleischer 1990; Jones 1994, 1995; Bond, Fleischer, and Wood 2003). Yet, the Chief Executive's formal role in this arena is actually quite small. For example, it is the subject of only 15 words in the Constitution[1]. Where there is a specific constitutional provision, as with the president's power to appoint federal officials, leadership is easily traceable. But in the legislative arena, the president acts with virtually no formal authority or guidance. Indeed, "[t]ransactional leadership is valued, transformational leadership is typically frustrated, and charismatic leadership is actively thwarted" in our system (Jones 2000). Thus, it is an area where presidential power is most surely the "power to persuade" (Neustadt 1960).

This pattern of power without formal authority raises two fundamental questions:

- Why did this come about?
- Without any formal power, how *does* the president lead?

Of the two questions, the first is largely historical and descriptive and is already widely explored (e.g., see Rossiter 1956, Wayne 1978, Cronin 1980, Sundquist 1981, and Edwards and Wayne 2003). The second question is less well understood and requires a more analytical answer. For one thing, it assumes that we actually know when the president *is* leading. As will become clear later, this assumption is a dangerous one. It is based on the notion that what the president does is knowable. It is this second question of how the president leads and its related implications which drives the research of this project.

The task at hand requires a systematic analysis of presidential activity. Since, presumably, presidential fortunes are made and lost in the legislative arena ("One campaign commitment I considered essential", Jimmy Carter once said, "was my promise to work well with Congress." [Carter 1982]), a study which brings to light their activities, and does so in a systematic fashion, should prove a necessary prelude to the study of presidential power and influence within our political system.

Neustadt claims the president's formal powers amount to no more than that of a glorified clerkship, and real presidential power in *all* arenas lies in the ability to persuade. However, this theory of presidential power is unfortunately the victim of its own success and acceptance. In the years since the publication of *Presidential Power*, scholars often cited (in the last 30 years, there are literally hundreds of citations in the Social Sciences Citation Index), critiqued and reassessed it (e.g., see Cronin 1974, Rockman et al 1981, Shapiro et al 2000)[2]. What they rarely do is explore Neustadt's

---

[1] See Article II, Section 3

[2] There was an entire conference devoted to assessing Neustadt's work in November of 1996 at Columbia University in New York City.

theory in a systematic or analytic fashion (Polsby 1986; for some noteworthy exceptions, see Edwards 1980, 1989, Sullivan 1988, 1991); rather, it is damned by its acceptance and is not used to advance the study of the presidency. Herein lies the danger mentioned earlier: How can it be known if and when the president *attempts* to persuade (i.e. lead)? Yet it is apparent from much of the research mentioned that presidential activity matters (see also Covington, Wrighton, and Kinney 1995).

Empirically addressing the question of presidential leadership requires some sort of categorization and measurement of presidential activity. There is certainly precedent for considering this approach. The ability to empirically measure and categorize congressional activity in any number of ways (e.g., Miller and Stokes 1964, Fenno 1973, Mayhew 1974, Kingdon 1981, Price 1985, and Arnold 1990) undeniably adds to our understanding of Congress. Currently, while we can define congressional activity in terms of action in the legislative process (referral, hearings, markup sessions), and, of course, in analyzing floor votes, there exists no similar systematic categorization of presidential activity[3].

This project develops such a categorization of activities, including those actions designed to move congressional opinion closer to presidential opinion. In addition, the selection of these activities are modeled, focusing on those which are definably persuasive in nature. There are three questions to keep in mind: First, in what kinds of legislative activities do presidents engage? Second, what factors affect the activities presidents choose to pursue? Finally, are these categorized behaviors useful to presidential scholars?

Addressing these questions lays the groundwork for expanding Neustadt's idea of presidential power into a more fully and systematically empirical study. The data should help us to explore just what makes presidents persuasive (or powerful, or successful), and just what effect variables like status and authority (among a host of others) have on a president's behavior. Additionally, the data should allow us to pursue the second question by itself. In other words, we should be able to systematically explore the origins of presidential activity.

In addressing these two questions, it is clear that activity data are useful both as a dependent and an independent variable.

---

[3] Though not a complete assessment of presidential activities, one can get a sense of what is missing from not having such data by referring to Brace and Hinckley's (1993) study of the impact of presidential activities on Gallup approval ratings.

Chapter 2: Power and Influence

This chapter briefly examines two bodies of literature that are central to identifying legislative behaviors: theories of power and measures of influence. More important than their specific measures, models, or conclusions, this literature suggests something of the underlying conceptual structure necessary for studying presidential behavior. This chapter demonstrates how these studies suggest three central notions of power: change, differing predispositions toward action on the part of the actors involved, and attempts by one side to move the others' opinions towards their own.

Normative Studies of Power

The formal theory of power has a venerable history (see Nagel 1975). For example, at about the same time that Neustadt was formulating his ideas on presidential power a large number of studies focused on the content of "power" and how to measure it. Robert Dahl (1969) organized this literature into three basic types of power measures: "game-theoretical", "Newtonian", and "economic".

A game-theoretic measure is probably the most limited type. An example is Shapley and Shubik's (1954) "committee system" measure. Here, power is defined as the probability of casting the pivotal vote in a winning coalition.

The Newtonian (or "vector") measure has been the most commonly proposed. Here, power is measured essentially as "the amount of change in R attributable to C. The greater the change in R, the greater the power of C" (Dahl 1969; see also Simon 1957, March 1957, Dahl 1957, 1963, and Oppenheim 1961).

Economic measures build upon the Newtonian approach. Economic measures include "(1) the opportunity costs to C of attempting to influence R, . . . and (2) the opportunity costs to R of refusing to comply with C" (Harsanyi 1962).

Robert Dahl's work is the most notable tailored to political power. According to Dahl (1969)

> [t]he closest equivalent to the power relation is the causal relation. For the assertion "C has power over R," one can substitute the assertion, "C's behavior causes R's behavior."

For the purposes of this project, substitute "the President" for C, and "the Congress" for R. Thus, "the President has power over the Congress" if "the President's behavior causes the Congress's behavior." In a more formal sense, Dahl (1957) would describe presidential power as the difference between the probability of Congress taking certain actions in the presence of presidential behaviors and the probability of Congress taking those same actions without any presidential activity[4]. The "Dahl formula" seems the perfect basis on which to systematically examine Neustadt's idea of presidential power. Implicit in Dahl's argument and the Newtonian and economic concepts is that power is the ability to *change* behavior. Furthermore, it would make sense to say that this change must be "factional" or "partisan" change[5]. That is, the actor attempting the change is actively looking to alter the other actor's behavior. This altered behavior should be one *outside* the range of behaviors originally considered acceptable by the second actor. It is hardly an act of power to get an actor to shift from one acceptable behavior to another acceptable one. It is certainly an act of power to get that actor to shift from an acceptable behavior to one that was previously considered unacceptable. Finally, change requires that the actors involved have different predispositions toward action. Again it is hardly an act of power to get someone to do something they were already predisposed toward doing.

To sum, Dahl and the other power theorists provide the criteria for identifying "power" behaviors: they are those activities which enhance the

---

[4] In his 1957 article, we can derive the following formula

$$M = P(a,x/A,w) - P(a,x/A,\sim w)$$

Where **M** is the amount of power **A** has, and $P(a,x/A,w)$ is "the probability that **a** will do **x**, given action **w** by **A**" and $P(a,x/A,\sim w)$ is "the probability that **a** will do **x**, given no action by **A**." (p. 207).

[5] "Partisan" is not necessarily meant in its often used sense of referring to political party allegiances. Rather, it is used in the broader sense of simple philosophical or opinion allegiances.

president's ability to 1) change the behavior of some other actor; 2) act as a partisan for change; or 3) identify the normal predisposition of targeted members.

Measures of Influence

In a similar vein, there are numerous debates surrounding empirical studies of presidential influence in Congress. These are properly labeled as debates about measuring power according to the Newtonian definition. The most notable progenitor in this area is Aaron Wildavsky's (1966) "Two Presidencies" thesis. Wildavsky attempts to explain why presidents seemingly fared better at influencing the course of foreign policy than that of domestic policy. He based his definition of influence and his explanations on *Congressional Quarterly*'s (CQ) "Presidential Boxscore". This measure "determined how many specific legislative requests made in presidential messages to Congress and in other public statements during the calendar year were ultimately enacted into law" (Edwards 1980).

Most subsequent work used either Wildavsky's measure or some variant thereof. Variants included focusing on vote margin, "key" votes (as defined by CQ), and size of proposal (see especially Edwards 1985; also see LeLoup and Shull 1979, Sigelman 1979, Edwards 1978, 1980, and 1989, Cohen 1980, and Rivers and Rose 1985).

This type of reasoning subsequently came under fire from those who claim that these techniques do not measure influence, but simply the amount of agreement between the two branches caused by other factors (e.g., see Pritchard 1983, 1986, Sullivan 1988). For example, it may be the case that members of Congress and the president share policy preferences because they are recruited from the same segments of the population. This may then lead Congress to enact proposals favored by the president without the presence of any influence. This suggests that "influence" is more than agreement. The requirements of partisanship and differing predispositions are missing. Influence should consist of agreement where two actors are predisposed toward **dis**agreement (as is suggested in the power studies). Thus there is a serious question of validity when using only the CQ Boxscore, or any similar score of agreement between the two branches, to measure presidential "influence" (no matter which votes or proposals are considered).

To reduce the bias associated with such problems, recent research uses a stricter definition of influence. The basis for a more rigorous definition is actually quite well-established: it is Dahl's causal relationship noted earlier. Consider this passage on influence from his text, *Modern Political Analysis*[6]:

---

[6] In a slightly altered form, this originally appears in Dahl's 1957 discussion of power.

Suppose you were to stand on a street corner and say to yourself, "I command all automobile drivers on this street to drive on the right-hand side of the road"; suppose also that all the drivers on this street actually did as you "commanded" them to do. Most people would regard you as mentally ill if you were to insist that you had just shown enough influence over automobile drivers to compel them to use the right-hand side of the road. On the other hand, suppose a police officer stands in the middle of an intersection at which most traffic ordinarily moves ahead and orders all traffic to turn right or left rather than go ahead. The traffic moves right or left as ordered. Then common sense suggests that the officer acting in this particular role influences automobile drivers . . . (Dahl 1984).

The former case is not an example of influence whereas the latter case clearly is. The difference between the two seems to be the notion of one actor *causing* another actor to behave in a way that is *different* from what that actor would do otherwise.

Anita Pritchard (1983) notes that "the definition of influence . . . presumes that a [presidential] force has an impact or *makes a difference* in [congressional] voting decisions" (emphasis added). In a quite similar vein, Terry Sullivan (1988) points out that "[f]irst, *change over time* from one position to another must be identified. And second, changes associated with *conversion* [i.e., presidential influence] must be distinguished from changes which are merely the normal acting out of a member's own decision calculus exclusive of presidential input" (emphasis added). So, as with the earlier power studies, these empirical studies suggest that presidential legislative activities attempt to generate *partisan change*.

It seems that these empirical studies of presidential influence have much in common with the normative power studies. They both identify similar elements of what could constitute presidential legislative activities (as defined in the introduction of this project). First these behaviors must be designed to produce a change in congressional behavior. Second, they must be consciously geared toward altering congressional behavior in a direction not previously considered acceptable by Congress. And finally, implicit in that notion of non-acceptability is that there is an underlying difference in the predispositions of Congress and the president in that instance.

The Dahl formula is the key. Behavior is the independent variable. The effect of that behavior is the dependent variable. If the ultimate goal of this line of research is to see how the *president's* behavior can alter *Congress's* actions, then the most important step we must take is the first one: applying these concepts to identifying presidential legislative activities. Along the way, it is also valuable to pursue the causes of a president's behavior. This would presumably provide us with some predictive power — both in terms of presidential behavior itself, as well as on the 'success' of an administration.

Accomplishing any of this first requires a set of presidential activities to label as legislative or non-legislative. This, once again is the rationale for the development of activity data. Once compartmentalized, the above criteria may be used to categorize presidential activities as legislative or not.

Chapter 3: Categorizing Legislative Activities

Chapter 2 identified some general characteristics of legislative activities: those encompassing change, and a predisposition toward "partisan" differences. In this chapter a taxonomy of legislative activities is suggested. Ultimately, this taxonomy will accomplish two tasks: First, it will categorize the *type* of activities; and second, it will allow measurement of the *degree* to which each category is exhibited.

Type of Activity

Robert Dahl's studies of power and influence provide a very useful start. He suggests three "means of influence" (1984, 38-43). In this categorization, Dahl includes "training", rational or manipulative "persuasion", and "inducement". Since to Dahl, "training" refers to creating behavior through control in the Pavlovian sense, it is not directly appropriate for the present purposes[7]. This leaves two useful categories.

Persuasion (part of, but not to be confused with Neustadt's notion of persuasion), as Dahl defines it, is the use of facts and information to elicit a certain response. If the facts and information are truthful, then Dahl terms the persuasion "rational". A good example of this type of interaction is the professional-client conversation in which advice is received from a doctor or

---

[7] The possibility of placing Neustadt's (1960) concepts of "anticipated reactions", and the use of "professional reputation" under this category may be worth exploring. However, these two concepts do not strictly fit the definition of "training". Other categories which may be more amenable to the label of "training" are discussed below.

lawyer on how to act (Dahl 1984). Such conversations generally cover outcomes associated with an action, often in the form of a cost-benefit analysis. If the facts and information are unrelated, exaggerated, less than complete, or outright lies, then Dahl terms the persuasion "manipulative". Examples of manipulative persuasion may be often found in partisan speeches, and in some media advertisements. Additionally, appeals to such things as God, country, partisanship, elections, or emotions would fall under this category.

Inducement is defined by Dahl as altering the environment in order to elicit a certain response. As Dahl discusses it, this alteration could take two forms (not specifically mentioned by Dahl): positive and negative inducement. Positive inducement is best termed rewarding, bribery, or something very much akin to what Neustadt has in mind when he talks of "bargaining" (Neustadt 1960). For this project, it entails essentially the offering of favors to members of Congress which are not specifically associated with the actions at hand. Negative inducement is best called punishment, or what Dahl refers to as "coercion". This is basically threatening to withhold actions for, or take action against members of Congress in an area not specifically associated with the actions at hand. Dahl does mention a third method of inducement — physical force — which may reasonably be ruled out.

For current purposes, the above categories fall under a broader category of behavior best termed "Pitching". Pitches are essentially the options open to the president when deciding how best to get one or a few legislators to support the passage of any single piece of legislation. Pitches are generally limited to a one-on-one (or small group), short-run activity.

There are at least two other types of legislative activities in which the president may engage: *Organization*, and *Emphasis*. These may be grouped into another broad category akin to training (see footnote 7, above) — "Strategy".

Organization involves setting up rules and procedures with the goal of increasing the likelihood that any piece of presidentially-based legislation will be passed by Congress (see Walcott and Hult 1995). This involves such things as the size, strength, and activity of the Office of Management and Budget and the Office of Congressional Relations in their development of legislation and its presentation to Congress. Staffing, rule-making, and any standard practices or ad hoc directions set up for interacting with Congress are also part of organizing to the extent that their ultimate objective is the creation of future leverage (whether long-term or immediate).

Emphasis involves such things as the order of proposals submitted to Congress, when they are presented, and how much they are stressed or mentioned. Timing is an important element of Emphasis, as is agenda-setting. An example of an emphasis activity might be a discussion of whether or not to send budget cuts or tax cuts to Congress first in order to gather optimal support for both. Along the same lines, some questions involving Emphasis may be: Is it best to send a proposal to Congress right away, or to wait awhile? Does the president publicize and stress a proposal with a televised address, press conference, or some other high-profile forum, or does he let it lay low?

Dimensions

Clearly, these activities fall along at least two basic dimensions: *Temporal Focus*, i.e., whether the view is long-term, short-term or inter-mediate; and *Target*, i.e., whether contact is with a single individual legislator, a group, or the Congress as a whole. *Organization* is usually a long-run, Congressionally targeted activity. *Emphasis* is usually an inter-mediate, group or Congressionally targeted activity. The various *Pitches* noted before are usual short-run, group or individually targeted activity.

Amount of Activity

Not only is it important to know what kind of behavior the president engages in, but it is essential to assess how the president distributes time to these different behaviors. No matter what type of behavior is used, nor what results it produces, a president allocating little time to a proposal cannot be said to be exercising much power or influence in that area. Along the same lines, time allocation is an important indicator of the emphasis placed on various proposals. Finally, any relative comparisons of presidential power would need to account for time spent in legislative activities.

Discussion of Type and Amount

Many works provide well organized descriptive accounts of the degree and type of behaviors used by various executives in various instances (see especially Kingdon 1977, 1981, Wayne 1978, Edwards 1980, 1989, and Edwards and Wayne 2003). In general, these accounts lead one to believe that there is a case for recognizing the type and amount of behavior as important aspects of presidential leadership. George Edwards' (1980) work seems to provide much anecdotal evidence of the importance of the type and amount of presidential activity. Consider the following passages:

> The 1957 school construction bill failed by three votes as the Secretary of Health, Education and Welfare (HEW) waited for Eisenhower to make calls on its behalf. Republican forces tried to reach him to elicit a statement of his support after his support became the central issue of debate. On

several occasions the president had spoken the correct words in support of the school aid program advocated by HEW Secretary Marion Folsom but then withdrew from the political fray (p. 136).

On the 1964 tax cut, Johnson, after intensive personal lobbying within the Senate Finance Committee to reverse a vote on one of Senator Dirksen's amendments, sent word that he wanted no amendments on the Senate floor. Meanwhile, Senator Hubert Humphrey (soon to be vice president) was urging a change in the bill. Nevertheless, after a call from the White House, he voted against his own amendment (p. 125).

In the first instance, Eisenhower's never-materialized phone calls were hoped-for *pitches* designed to make up for an apparently low level of *emphasis* activity. It is clear that the behaviors noted (as being either present or absent-but-desired) are indeed legislative activities. They are designed to produce "partisan" change in a Congress that is predisposed (in the aggregate) towards voting against the president. The second instance is clearly a short-run, individually targeted (and apparently effective!) *Pitch*.

Chapter 4: Gathering the Data

For each president studied, the research task is to chronicle and categorize the president's activities — and most importantly, his "legislative activities" — for a specified period of time.

Sources of Presidential Activity Data

The most profitable sources of data on presidential activity are found in presidential libraries. There are many useful files available in most presidential libraries. Given the range of "researchable" presidents (those with complete enough records to analyze meaningfully, which is essentially from Eisenhower through Carter — though with the advent of computerized record-keeping, the Reagan and Bush administrations are rapidly catching up to the others), Dwight Eisenhower, Lyndon Johnson, and Richard Nixon present some of the most notable contrasts in style, personality, and activity. In addition, there are useful differences among them in party, ideology, and Congressional leadership. As such, these three presidents represent the most parsimonious selection of "researchable" presidential administrations.

The database of presidential activity is comprised of a minute by minute accounting of sample periods of the administrations of Eisenhower, Johnson, and Nixon. The samples are drawn from the first, second, and fourth years following their first election to office[8]. They run from January 20th through May 19th of these years — a one-third sample of each year. The data on each president are gathered from their respective presidential libraries, relying mainly on the presidential diaries (known in the Eisenhower Library

---

[8] Again, parsimony was the guide. These years cover a non-election year, a congressional election year, and a presidential election year, respectively. In addition, the first year covers just that: an initial year — the first 'go-round' for each administration.

Dwight Eisenhower (Library of Congress)

Lyndon Johnson (Yoichi Okamoto, LBJ Library)

Richard Nixon (Library of Congress)

as the DDE Diary Series, and in the Johnson Library and Nixon Project as the Daily Diary). These are not to be confused with personal diaries. They are more like detailed appointment logs, recording the president's movements, his visitors, his meetings, phone calls, and travels. In essence, these files provide the best assessment of exactly what the president does on a day to day basis. They contain the president's "Daily Diary sheets, which log appointments and phone calls . . . and a Diary backup file of schedules, memoranda, and lists for each day's appointments . . ." (HISTORICAL MATERIALS 1988). These data are fleshed out with information drawn from many other files, including the files of various staff members, some cabinet secretaries, and records of standard meetings like Cabinet and National Security Council meetings. In all, they make it quite possible to discern the type and amount of presidential activities with a fair degree of precision. Chapter 5 provides a detailed look at sample documents and how they were coded for purposes of this study.

Much of the information for the Eisenhower sample (including the DDE Diary Series) was drawn from what has become known as the *Ann Whitman File*. Ann Whitman was Eisenhower's personal secretary during his tenure in the White House.

These are the President's office files, maintained during his administration by his personal secretary, Ann Whitman. The documents in this collection . . . include the President's correspondence and memoranda, agenda, press releases, reports and other materials documenting the . . . political activities of the President and his associates, and the President's personal affairs (HISTORICAL MATERIALS 1989, p. 86).

Included in this file are: the *Ann Whitman Diary Series*, which helps to supplement the president's diary; the *Cabinet Series* which contains detailed notes of every cabinet meeting held, including summaries and often quotes of the discussions that took place in these meetings; and the *Legislative Meetings* and *NSC Series* which provide equally detailed notes of the regular meetings with the legislative leadership and the National Security Council. Each of these helped to add considerable detail to the diary.

Use of the diary is further supplemented by various name files including, but not limited to: Arthur Minnich, the Assistant White House Staff Secretary; Bryce Harlow, Special Assistant for Congressional Relations; and Wilton Persons, Assistant to the President.

The information for the Johnson sample stems mainly from the *Daily Diary* and *Diary Backup*. These were supplemented by the *Cabinet Papers* and the

National Security Meetings files which contained notes on the meetings of these groups. These and other meetings are also contained in the *Meeting Notes* file.

The files of various personnel also supplemented the Johnson data. They include, but are not limited to: Bill Moyers, Special Assistant to the President; Lawrence O'Brien, Special Assistant for Congressional Relations; George Reedy, Press Secretary; Juanita Roberts, Personal Secretary; and Marvin Watson, Special Assistant to the President.

The Nixon data was similarly drawn from the *Daily Diary*. The Nixon administration kept what they referred to as a *Record Copy* and a *File Copy* of the Diary. These are analogous to Johnson's Diary and Backup, respectively. They were supplemented by other files including the *President's Office Files*, the *President's Personal Files*, the *Meeting Notes File*, and the *Chronological File*.

The personnel files further used include those of Rosemary Woods, the president's personal secretary; John Ehrlichman, Special Assistant to the President for Domestic Affairs; H.R. Haldeman, Special Assistant to the President; Dwight Chapin, Appointment Secretary; and Alexander Butterfield, Deputy Assistant to the President for White House Operations.

Presidential Diaries provide a surprisingly complete record of the president's days. The entries cover not only workday activity in the Oval office, but also social, and personal activity in the residence as well as activity outside the White House. In Figures 4-1 and 4-2 (below), note that President Eisenhower's lunch and dinner schedule and companions are noted; and that President Nixon's breakfast and dinner times are recorded as well as his personal interactions with his family.

There is always the question of accuracy to consider. However, while presidents whose minds may be focussed on the history books may want to see only the positive aspects of their administration remembered, there is no evidence that they undertook any *major* steps towards this end. When one finds, for example, records of Lyndon Johnson agreeing to the harassment of the family of an 'uncooperative' legislator (see Figure 5-2 in Chapter 5, below), one is inclined to believe that editing (for whatever reason) was not a high priority of the record-keepers. Historian Michael Beschloss (1997) notes that Johnson wanted recently-uncovered tapes of his phone calls concealed — some for 50 years, others forever. If a president's goal is to manipulate history, why hide the data?

In addition, there is reason to believe that presidents *wanted* and *benefited* from accurate records of their activities. An accurate record of discussions with members of Congress or with leading corporate figures or policy advocates can prove quite beneficial to a president seeking to develop and implement a legislative program. To that end, the Johnson administration kept a separate file on each member of Congress, for example, and Nixon gave standing orders early on for his aides to turn in a prepared summary of every meeting they attended with him.

Coding the Data

Each diary entry is coded as a single activity (with some exceptions which are explained below). They are coded for the following variables: Where, within and outside of the White House, the actions occurred was coded as its *Location*. The main distinction within this variable is between the president's "Residence" and "Office". Other rooms within the White House (such as the "State Dining Room" or the "East Room" are noted as well. Locations outside the White House are coded by place name (such as "New York" or "Baltimore") unless specific places or buildings (Such as "Rose Garden", "LBJ Ranch", or "Camp David") are usefully identified. Travel is coded as such. That is to say, automotive travel is designated "Road", rail travel is designated "Train", and air travel is designated as either being by "Helicopter" or by the presidential plane ("Columbine" for Eisenhower, "AF-1" for Johnson, and "AF-1" or "Spirit of '76" for Nixon).

The *Date* is coded simply by assigning consecutive numbers to each succeeding day[9]. The beginning and ending *Times* of each activity are coded in the 24 hour, four digit format usually referred to as "military time". In addition, the *Duration* of each activity is recorded in minutes.

Time and *Duration* require further explanation. These observations are by where the president's attention is immediately focused. As a result, there are more observations in the dataset than there are diary entries. This occurs because shifts in attention or changes in the structure of an activity are coded as new observations. For example, if a meeting is interrupted by a phone call, the dataset contains an observation for the initial portion of the meeting, for the phone call, and for the resumption of the meeting (i.e., three activities instead of two). Also if people arrive at or leave a meeting serially instead of all at once (or if people wander in and out of a meeting), one observation is recorded for each consecutive combination of meeting participants (so a single meeting may have a number of different entries in the dataset as people enter and exit). Finally, idle or unrecorded times are also included as observations. For example, if a diary entry shows a meeting ending at noon, and the next entry is for a phone call placed at 12:05 pm, the dataset includes not only those two activities, but also the idle time from 12:00 pm to 12:05 pm as well.

---

[9] The numbering scheme used in the database comes from the @**DATE** function in the *Lotus 1-2-3* spreadsheet program. This function assigns the number 1 to January 1st, 1900, and numbers each successive day consecutively. For example, January 20th 1953 is coded as 19379, meaning that it is 19,379 days after January 1st 1900.

Figure 4-1: Sample Daily Diary — Eisenhower

THE PRESIDENT'S APPOINTMENTS
FRIDAY, MAY 1, 1953

8:10 am   (Colonel Paul Carroll) OFF THE RECORD

8:20 am   (General Wilton B. Persons) OFF THE RECORD

8:30 am   Congressman Walter H. Judd, Minnesota
(The Congressman called Mr. Stephens yesterday, to say he had
just returned from a trip to India, and would like to come in
and discuss it with the President.)

9:00 am   Monsignor Edward E. Swanstrom, Executive Director, National Catholic
Welfare Conference, War Relief Services
Dr. Walter W. VanKirk, Executive Director, National Council of the
Churches of Christ in the U. S. A., Department of International
Justice and Goodwill
Dr. Paul C. Empie, Executive Director, National Lutheran Council
Mr. Walter Bierringer, President, United Service for New Americans
(with approval of other National Jewish organizations)
Mr. Roland Elliott, Director, Immigration Services, Church and
World Services
(This group from the National Council of the Churches of Christ,
requested the appointment in order to discuss with the President
the Immigration Law and policies and to urge enactment of an
emergency immigration law.)

9:30 am   (Mr. and Mrs. Patrick Breslin of Belle Mar, New Jersey) OFF THE RECORD
(Congressman Auchincloss asked Mr. Stephens to let these people
come to his office and then run then in for an OFF THE RECORD
handshake.)

9:35 am   Senator H. Alexander Smith, New Jersey

9:45 am   (Honorable Richard Nixon, The Vice President)
(Mayor John Butler, San Diego, California) OFF THE RECORD
(The Vice President asked if he might take Mayor Butler in to
see the President prior to Cabinet)

10:00 am Cabinet Meeting
Hon. Richard Nixon, The Vice President
Hon. John Foster Dulles, The Secretary of State
Hon. George M. Humphrey, The Secretary of the Treasury
Hon. Marion B. Folsom, Under Secretary of the Treasury
Hon. Roger Kyes, Acting Secretary of Defense
Hon. Herbert Brownell, The Attorney General
Hon. Arthur Summerfield, The Postmaster General
Hon. Douglas McKay, The Secretary of the Interior
Hon. Ezra Taft Benson, The Secretary of Agriculture
Hon. Sinclair Weeks, The Secretary of Commerce
Hon. Martin Durkin, The Secretary of Labor
Hon. Oveta Culp Hobby, The Secretary of Health, Education & Welfare

FRIDAY, MAY 1, 1953   Page 2

10:00   Cabinet (Continued)
           Hon. Henry Cabot Lodge, Ambassador to UN
           Hon. Joseph Dodge, Director, Bureau of the Budget
           Hon. Harold Stassen, Director for Mutual Security
           Hon. Philip Young, Chairman, Civil Service Commission
           Hon. Val Peterson, Administrator, Civil Defense
           Hon. Robert Cutler
           Hon. Sherman Adams
           Hon. Bernard Shanley
           General Wilton B. Persons
           Mr. Gerald Morgan
           Hon. Emmet Hughes
           Mr. Arthur Minnich

12:30 pm   Congressman James C. Auchincloss, New Jersey
           Congressman J. Harry McGregor, Ohio
           (Congressman Auichincloss called Mr. Stephens and asked if they
           might call on the President before next Tuesday, to discuss
           the St. Lawrence Seaway.)

1:00 pm   (Governor Dan Thornton, Colorado) OFF THE RECORD
           (Governor Thornton came to the Executive Offices and walked
           over to the White House with President for lunch.)

2:30 pm   Honorable Ellsworth Bunker, former American Ambassador to Italy
           (Mr. Bunker asked for this thru Division of Protocol, to pay
           respects. General "Beetle" Smith suggested the President
           talk to him about his interest in Latin America, as he thought
           Bunker might be of some help to Dr. Milton Eisenhower on his trip)

2:45 pm   (Honorable Sherman Adams)
           (General Carl Gray, Administrator of Veterans Affairs)
           (Honorable W. Randolph Burgess, Deputy Secretary of the Treasury)
           (Honorable Gabriel Hauge)
           (Mr. Gerald Morgan)
           (OFF THE RECORD - Arranged at the suggestion of Governor
           Adams, to discuss rates on FHA and veterans loans)

3:15 pm   Honorable Harry McDonald, Chairman, Reconstruction Finance Corporation
           (Mr. McDonald came in to pay his respects and say goodbye)

3:20 pm   Honorable Kenneth Royall, former Secretary of the Army

4:00 pm   (Dr. Milton Eisenhower) OFF THE RECORD

4:30 pm   (Hon. John Foster Dulles, Secretary of State)
           (Hon. Roger Kyes, Acting Secretary of Defense) OFF THE RECORD
           (Gen. Hoyt S. Vandenberg, for J. C. S)

5:00 pm   (Dr. Milton Eisenhower) OFF THE RECORD
           (Dr. Eisenhower walked over to the White House with the President
           and remained for dinner)

Figure 4-2: Sample Daily Diary — Nixon

THE WHITE HOUSE			PRESIDENT RICHARD NIXON'S DAILY DIARY	
			(See Travel Record for Travel Activity)	

PLACE DAY BEGAN				DATE (Mo., Day, Yr.)
				MAY 4, 1970
				TIME DAY
THE WHITE HOUSE – WASHINGTON, D.C.				8:20 MONDAY

TIME		PHONE P=Placed R=Received		ACTIVITY
In	Out	Lo	LD	
8:20				The President had breakfast.
8:30				The President went to his office.
8:35	10:55			The President met with:
9:05	9:24			H.R. Haldeman, Assistant
9:19	11:08			John D. Ehrlichman, Assistant
10:10	10:44			Henry A. Kissinger, Assistant
				Ronald L. Ziegler, Press Secretary
11:12	11:40			The President met with:
11:23	11:24			H.R. Haldeman, Assistant
				Ronald L. Ziegler, Press Secretary
11:41				The President went to his EOB office.
11:42	11:43	P		The President talked with his Assistant, John D. Ehrlichman
11:43		P		The President telephoned his Assistant, Henry A. Kissinger. The call was not completed.
11:50	11:53			The President met with:
11:50	1:08			Henry A. Kissinger, Assistant
12:55	1:35			John D. Ehrlichman, Assistant
				Henry A. Kissinger, Assistant
1:24	1:28	P		The President talked with his Press Sectretary, Ronald L. Ziegler.
2:48	2:53			The President met with his Deputy Assistant, Alexander P. Butterfield.
2:56	2:57	P		The President talked with his Assistant, H.R. Haldeman.
3:00	4:38			The President met with his Assistant, H.R. Haldeman.
4:39	4:46	P		The President talked with his Assistant, Henry A. Kissinger.
4:50	5:11			The President met with NSC staff member, Alexander M. Haig.
5:08			P	The President telephoned long distance to General Maxwell Taylor, in Florence, Alabama. The call was not completed.
5:10	5:13	P		The President talked with his Assistant, H.R. Haldeman.
5:17		P		The President telephoned his Press Secretary, Ronald L. Ziegler. The call was not completed.
5:19		P		The President telephoned his Special Counsel, Harry S. Dent. The call was not completed.

| THE WHITE HOUSE | PRESIDENT RICHARD NIXON'S DAILY DIARY |
| (See Travel Record for Travel Activity) | |

PLACE DAY BEGAN

THE WHITE HOUSE - WASHINGTON, D.C.

DATE (Mo., Day, Yr.)
MAY 4, 1970

| TIME | DAY |
| 5:23 | MONDAY |

TIME		PHONE P=Placed R=Received		ACTIVITY
In	Out	Lo	LD	
5:23	5:26	R		The President talked with his Press Secretary, Ronald L. Ziegler.
5:23	6:14			The President met with his Assistant, Henry A. Kissinger.
5:26	5:32	R		The President talked with his Special Counsel, Harry S. Dent.
5:47	5:57	R		The President talked with his Assistant, H.R. Haldeman.
6:14				The President, accompanied by his Assistant, Henry A. Kissinger, went to the second floor of the Residence.
6:28	6:34	P		The President talked with his Assistant, H.R. Haldeman.
6:41				Assistant Henry A. Kissinger departed.
6:43	6:45	P		The President talked with his Assistant, H.R. Haldeman.
6:50	6:53	P		The President talked with his Assistant, H.R. Haldeman.
7:00				The President had dinner with: The First Lady Patricia Nixon
7:14	7:20	P		The President talked with his Assistant, H.R. Haldeman.
7:55	8:07			The President and his daughter, Patricia, went to the South Grounds of the White House and then returned.
8:06		R		The President was telephoned by his Assistant, Henry A. Kissinger. The call was not completed.
8:12	8:34	R		The President talked with his Assistant, Henry A. Kissinger.
8:40	8:45	P		The President talked with his Special Counsel, Harry S. Dent.
9:19	9:28	P		The President talked with his Assistant, Henry A. Kissinger.
9:28	9:35		P	The President talked long distance with his daughter, Julie Eisenhower, in Massachusetts.
9:47	10:06	P		The President talked with his Assistant, H.R. Haldeman.

There are two further variables, for which each observation is coded: the *Medium* and *Type* of activity. These require a somewhat more detailed description.

Medium refers to the method of the interaction or activity. A face-to-face interaction is coded as a "Meeting"; Phone calls placed by the president are coded as "Outgoing Phone calls", call to the president are coded as "Incoming Phone calls"; "Speeches" are also coded. All others are coded as "Activities".

The final variable, *Type* refers to something similar to Clinton Rossiter's 'hats'. The question answered in coding for *Type* is basically, "In what capacity is the president acting?" There are five different possible *Types*: "Executive", "Legislative", "Foreign Policy/Diplomatic", "Social/Ceremonial", and "Personal". The "Executive" and "Personal" categories are 'fallback' positions and the others involve more specific criteria. Any interaction consisting solely of contact with members of the immediate presidential family, and any activity whose Location is coded as "Residence" and is not further definable is coded as a "Personal" activity (for a similar coding of personal activity, see Thompson 1991). Interactions with a member of the foreign policy establishment (such as the secretaries of State and Defense), including ambassadors (both US and foreign) are coded as "Foreign Policy/Diplomatic". "Social/Ceremonial" activities consist of items such as state dinners, bill signing ceremonies, photo and publicity opportunities, meetings described as a person or group 'paying their respects' to the president and the like. In addition, activities with people outside of government considered to be friends of the president, and gatherings with associates and their families are coded this way.

Since project focus is on presidential activity in the legislative arena, a further discussion of the "Legislative" type is necessary. "Legislative" activities are defined as essentially attempts to influence Congress. They are further subdivided into Pitches, as in sales pitches, and Strategic activities. As discussed in the previous chapter, Pitches involve what Robert Dahl (1984) defines as influence: verbal persuasion; and inducement (as in rewards or punishments). Strategic activities involve emphasizing or ordering proposals, and organizing the environment. To code observations as "Legislative", they need to meet rather strict standards. In brief, they need to be clearly documented as actions designed to move congressional opinion closer to presidential opinion. As such, there will be a tendency towards understating legislative activities. This conservative stance means that any significant findings regarding them are more likely to be true than to be any sort of artifact (see Chapter 7, below).

All other activities, including contacts with what Barber (1985) refers to as the "Washington establishment", undefinable activities in the Oval Office, and activities outside the White House that do not meet any of the other Type criteria are coded as "Executive" activities.

Chapter 5: Coding the Data — Some Detailed Examples

Any sort of content analysis is haunted by the lurking dangers of subjectivity — the social scientist's nemesis. Is the coding of the documents used reflective of some true underlying scheme, or is it merely reflective of the whims of the coder?

The dataset used for this project is way too large to lay open in its entirety for inspection in this book[10]. However, sample documents may certainly be presented as evidence of proper and useful coding.

After having described the coding scheme in the previous chapter, this chapter provides some actual examples of how documents are coded. The examples include selections from two typical days — one each from Presidents Eisenhower and Nixon (see Figures 4-1 and 4-2 above), and documents containing examples of each type of legislative behavior (since legislative behaviors are the most important types in this study). Examples from the three presidents in the dataset will be used to illustrate the six separate types of legislative behaviors (rational persuasion, manipulative persuasion, positive inducement, negative inducement, organization, and emphasis).

Typical Coding

Presidential diaries (the DDE Diary Series, and the Johnson and Nixon Daily Diaries) provided the backbone of the database. This section provides examples of how Diary entries were actually coded into the dataset. For the original Diaries, refer to Figures 4-1 and 4-2, above. There is one example

---

[10] The number of cases in the dataset exceeds 51,000. The SPSS data file consumes over 9 megabytes of disk space.

from the Eisenhower Administration (May 1st, 1953), and one from the
Nixon Administration (May 4, 1970). One major reason for demonstrating
how Diary entries are converted into database entries is noted in Chapter 4:
the Diary entries are not coded into the database on a one-to-one basis. One
other thing to note is that not all of the basic information coded into the
dataset comes from the Diaries. Documents like Secret Service location
records and White House phone records are used to fill out the data. Other
supplemental materials are noted in Chapter 4.

Non-controversial Diary entries are coded in a more or less
straightforward manner. For example, the first two entries in Eisenhower's
day are a meeting with Col. Paul Carroll, who then served as White House
Staff Secretary and Defense Liaison Officer, and a meeting with Gen.
Wilton Persons, who was a Deputy Assistant to the President. It reads as
follows:

8:10 am   (Colonel Paul Carroll)   OFF THE RECORD
8:20 am   (General Wilton B. Persons)   OFF THE RECORD

Those entries are translated into the database entries which are partly
depicted in Table 5-1:

Table 5-1: Abridged Database Entries For Eisenhower Sample

Location	Medium	Date	StHr[a]	StMn[b]	FiHr[c]	FiMn[d]	Type	Case	Time
Office	M	19840	8	10	8	20	E	Col. P Carrol (OR)	10
Office	M	19480	8	20	8	30	E	Persons (OR)	10

[a]StHr = Starting Hour
[b]StMn = Starting Minute
[c]FiHr = Finishing Hour
[d]FiMn = Finishing Minute

Reading the across the table, it says that both of these activities occurred
in the Oval Office; they were both meetings; they occurred on what translates
to May 1st, 1953 (see Footnote 9 in Chapter 4 for the discussion of date
coding); they both started during the 8 am hour; the first meeting started at 10
minutes past 8 am, while the second meeting started at 20 minutes past the
hour; they both ended during the 8 am hour; the first meeting ended at 20
minutes after 8, while the second meeting ended at half-past 8 am; they are
both coded as Executive activities (see Chapter 4 for a detailed explanation of
this particular coding scheme); the first meeting involved Col. Paul Carroll
and was Off the Record, while the second meeting was with Gen. Wilton

Persons and was also Off the Record; and finally, they both lasted 10 minutes. There are a number of other variables coded in the dataset, but these are the basics.

The first few entries in the Nixon record are as follows:

In	Out	Activity
8:20		The President had breakfast.
8:30		The President went to his office.
		The President met with:
8:35	10:55	H.R. Haldeman, Assistant
9:05	9:24	John D. Ehrlichman, Assistant
9:19	11:08	Henry A. Kissinger, Assistant
10:10	10:44	Ronald L. Ziegler, Press Secretary

Those entries are translated into the database entries which are partly depicted in Table 5-2:

Table 5-2: Abridged Database Entries For Nixon Sample

Location	Medium	Date	StHr[a]	StMn[b]	FiHr[c]	FiMn[d]	Type	Case	Time
Residence	A	25692	8	20	8	30	P	Breakfast	10
Office	A	25692	8	30	8	35	E	Office	5
Office	M	25692	8	35	9	5	E	Hald	30
Office	M	25692	9	5	9	19	E	Hald, Ehrl: Schedule	14
Office	M	25692	9	19	9	24	FP	Hald, Ehrl, Kiss	5
Office	M	25692	9	24	10	10	FP	Hald, Kiss	46
Office	M	25692	10	10	10	44	FP	Hald, Kiss, Zieg	34
Office	M	25692	10	44	10	55	FP	Hald, Kiss	11
Office	M	25692	10	55	11	8	FP	Kiss	13

[a]StHr = Starting Hour
[b]StMn = Starting Minute
[c]FiHr = Finishing Hour
[d]FiMn = Finishing Minute

Here we see clearly that the database is not a literal translation of the Diary entries. The first two entries in the Diary are entered into the database in a direct manner: President Nixon had breakfast in the White House Residence from 8:20 am to 8:30 am, at which time he headed to the Oval Office. He then spent 5 minutes there alone before meeting with several assistants for the next 2½ hours. It is here where the literal entries stop. While there are only four entries in the Diary, there are seven entries in the database. This is because the four Diary entries are not simply people entering and exiting the Oval Office serially. There are several overlaps, where more than one person is in the office with the president at a time. H.R. Haldeman was in the Oval Office with Nixon for most of that time, while John Ehrlichman, Henry Kissinger, and Press Secretary Ron Zeigler came and went. According to other documents, the meeting began with Haldeman and Ehrlichman reviewing the day's schedule with Nixon. These entries are coded as Executive activities. When Kissinger enters the office, the coding changes to Foreign Policy activities.

One final note about basic entries: As noted earlier, the Diaries offer a base upon which to build the database; but there *are* some entries in the database that came from records other than the Diaries. For example, part of the Eisenhower Diary reads as follows:

9:35 am   Senator H. Alexander Smith, New Jersey

9:45 am   (Honorable Richard Nixon, The Vice President)
            (Mayor John Butler, San Diego, California)
            OFF THE RECORD
            (The Vice President asked if he might take mayor Butler in to
            see the President prior to Cabinet)

However, examining the White House phone records revealed a phone call placed by Eisenhower right before the meeting with the Vice President and Mayor Butler, so the database contains entries, not only for the meetings with Senator Smith, and the Vice President and the Mayor, but also for the phone call, as noted in Table 5-3:

Table 5-3: Abridged Database Entries For Second Eisenhower Sample

Location	Medium	Date	StHr[a]	StMn[b]	FiHr[c]	FiMn[d]	Type	Case	Time
Office	M	19480	9	35	9	44	EC	Sen. HA Smith	9
Office	OP	19480	9	44	9	45	S	Larmon: Come visit	1
Office	M	19480	9	45	10	0	E	VP,SD Mayor Butler OR	15

[a]StHr = Starting Hour
[b]StMn = Starting Minute
[c]FiHr = Finishing Hour
[d]FiMn = Finishing Minute

The database reflects a meeting occurring with Senator Smith, from 9:35 am to 9:44 am. Its Type is coded as "EC", meaning it is an Executive activity with a member of Congress. There is no evidence of Legislative activity, so it is not coded as such, but since it involves a member of Congress, its Type is coded differently from other Executive activities.

The next activity is the phone call to Sigur Larmon, a member of the U.S. Information Agency as well as an old friend and supporter of Eisenhower's. The Medium is "OP" for Outgoing Phone call, and the Type is coded as Social/Ceremonial, since the phone records indicate that it is merely an invitation to visit the White House, and apparently does not contain any discussion of business.

Finally, the meeting with the Vice President and the Mayor of San Diego occurs and is recorded in the database in a straightforward manner.

So, the Presidential Diaries provide a firm foundation for the database. However, the database is not a simple recounting of the Diaries. It contains entries culled from other sources, and reflects greater degree of complexity in the president's focus than may be captured by the Diaries.

Persuasion

Recall that persuasion is the use of facts and information to elicit a certain response. *Rational* persuasion is the use of presumably truthful facts and information — often in the form of a cost-benefit analysis. *Manipulative* persuasion is the use of unrelated, exaggerated, or untruthful information — often in the form of appeals to such things as God, country, partisanship, or emotions.

Examples of Persuasive Behavior may be found throughout the dataset. One such example comes from the DDE Diary Series. It lists a meeting between President Eisenhower and the Congressional Leadership occurring on March 29th 1954, from 8:30am to 10:15am. Figure 5-1 (below) is a memo detailing the conference. This memo is contained in the first box of Legislative Meetings Files found at the Eisenhower Library. The memo provides examples of both types of persuasive activities. There are several references to Eisenhower's participation in the meetings. He "stressed", "urged", "indicated", "noted", and "discussed" various items on the policy agenda of the time. Persuasion is clearly evident in the first two items in the memo, public housing and agricultural research. The president is attempting to get his way on these two items by essentially telling congressional leaders what he feels is best to do in these areas. Since it appears that the president is sticking to the facts, these are coded as instances of rational persuasion. Later on, in discussing trade legislation, there are more instances of rational persuasion when "[t]he President noted the possibility of transactions which would result in net advantage to the United States."

On the other hand, persuasion of a different sort is apparent near the end of the memo. There is an appeal from the president to pass legislation, but the rationale is not connected to the benefits of that legislation. It seems the rationale is much more political in nature:

> The President discussed his forthcoming public addresses and urged that action on the broad Administration program be expedited in every possible way in order to give the addresses maximum effect.

The rationale for action here is not related to the benefits of the programs themselves, but rather to the "effect" passage will lend to the president's "forthcoming public addresses". As such, this passage clearly meets the definition of manipulative persuasion laid out earlier.

There are approximately 55 lines in the memo devoted to the legislative conference. Of these, about 4 lines are devoted to rational persuasion: two lines regarding public housing; one line regarding agricultural research; and one line regarding foreign economic policy. There are approximately 3 lines in the section on foreign economic policy (quoted above) devoted to manipulative persuasion. Given a meeting length recorded in the diary as 105 minutes, these numbers mean (assuming an even distribution of time throughout the document) the president spent roughly eight minutes engaged in rational persuasion and roughly six minutes engaged in manipulative persuasion.

Inducement

Recall that Inducement is altering the environment in order to elicit a certain response. *Positive* inducement is akin to rewarding, or bribery. For purposes of this project, it entails essentially the offering of favors to members of Congress which are not specifically associated with the actions at hand. *Negative* inducement is best called punishment. This is basically threatening to withhold actions for, or take action against members of Congress in an area not specifically associated with the actions at hand.

Negative Inducement (or punishment) is illustrated in Figure 5-2. This is a memo to President Johnson from White House aide Douglass Cater dated March 30, 1965. It was in Box 6 of the Handwriting Files at the Johnson Library. It contains suggestions for retaliation against a contrary member of Congress, Representative Edith Green (D-OR). This specific incident was recounted elsewhere by Joseph Califano:

Figure 5-1: Memo From Eisenhower Staff Secretary Minnich To Budget Director Joseph Dodge

THE WHITE HOUSE
WASHINGTON

March 30, 1954

PERSONAL AND CONFIDENTIAL

MEMORANDUM FOR: Mr. Dodge

The following notes on yesterday morning's Legislative Conference
may be of use to you:

Public Housing - The President stressed the need for approving without reducing the Administration's recommendation of 35,000 public
housing units for fiscal 1955, and Representative Halleck indicated
he would confer with Chairman Taber for that purpose.

Agricultural Research - The President urged that efforts be made to
prevent reduction of the Agricultural research appropriation.

Counter-Cyclical Program - Representative Halleck gave assurance that
the House would move quickly to accomplish the list of items in the
Administration program which Dr. Burns had designated as being particularly important to counter-cyclical action. The list included
housing, hospital construction, highway, unemployment insurance, St.
Lawrence Seaway, and tanker construction programs.

Highway Legislation - The President indicated that the Administration
may later request that this legislation take effect as soon as approved.
Senator Ferguson hoped that the amount to be authorized might be increased.

Hawaiian-Alaskan Statehood - Senator Knowland expected that this legislation would be approved by the Senate probably by Wednesday. Representative Halleck expressed doubts as to whether Alaskan statehood
could be separated and rejected either in Conference or in the House.

Foreign Economic Policy Message - The message was to be revised in
keeping with certain suggestions at this conference and be transmitted
to the Congress on March 30th.

In the course of the discussion, Senator Knowland ascertained that the
provision relating to cases of substandard wages in foreign countries
did not preclude consideration of normal wage differentials in the
negotiation of tariff agreements.

To Mr. Dodge, March 30, 1954 - page 2

Senators Knowland and Saltonstall and Speaker Martin made reference to domestic unemployment and expressed serious concern over the implications of the proposals regarding the Buy American Act.

Senator Millikin and Representative Dan Reed questioned the advisability of any reference to relaxation of restrictions on trade even in non-strategic items with Communist states. The President noted the possibility of transactions which would result in net advantage to the United States.

Senator Millikin, Speaker Martin, and Representatives Halleck and Reed cited the need for real reciprocity.

Because of its controversial nature, Senator Millikin seriously questioned the advisability of opening the foreign economic policy issue by any Presidential message at this time. Representative Halleck recalled that Congress had established the Randall Commission, that it was the President's duty to transmit recommendations, and that reactions tot he message could be assessed with a view to subsequent action. Both he and Senator Millikin characterized this issue as perhaps the most difficult to be faced by Congress. The President expected that objections to some of the recommendations would inevitably be voiced by members of Congress who usually support the Administration. Senator Knowland regarded some changes as inevitable but hoped they would not be too extensive.

Achievement of Administration Program - The President discussed his forthcoming public addresses and urged that action on the broad Administration program be expedited in every possible way in order to give the addresses maximum effect. Representative Halleck agreed on the need for accomplishing the entire program and predicted that the House would approve the Housing bill and anti-communist legislation this week, that amendment of the Taft-Hartley act would be done next week, and that the St. Lawrence Seaway legislation would be reported by the Rules committee also next week.

> L.A. Minnich, Jr.
> Assistant Staff Secretary

Distribution
> Mr. Shanley
> Gen. Persons
> Mrs. Whitman
> Mr. Morgan
> Dr. Hauge
> Mr. Willis
> Gen. Carroll
> Mr. Rabb

[There were problems the White House] was having with Edith Green, the irascible Democratic congresswoman from Oregon who chaired a key house education subcommittee. Green was trying to torpedo the administration's program to encourage innovative elementary and secondary education programs (Califano 1991).

The presidential activity itself comes at the bottom of the memo, where Johnson, in a handwritten note (shown in Figure 5-2 below in quotes and bold type), OKs the recommended actions to be taken against Rep. Green. The actions taken clearly fit the description of Negative Inducement laid out in Chapter 3. Nowhere are the merits of either the Higher Education Bill or Rep. Green's actions discussed. This was coded in the dataset as one minute (a standard for all notes and letters of one page or less in length) of Negative Inducement.

Figure 5-2: Memo From Douglass Cater To Lyndon Johnson

MEMORANDUM
                                THE WHITE HOUSE
                                WASHINGTON

                                                March 30, 1965

TO: THE PRESIDENT
FROM: Douglass Cater

Adam Clayton Powell is burning mad over Edith Green's behavior on the Education Bill. He has threatened three reprisals:

1. Remove vocational rehabilitation from her Subcommittee jurisdiction.

2. Fire her sister from the Committee staff.

3. Entrust John Brademas with sponsorship of the Higher Education Bill.

Brademas is uncertain about No. 3, but is willing to undertake the job if it will serve the good of the Bill.

"D
OK all 3
L"

Positive Inducement (or rewarding, reinforcement, or bribery) can be illustrated using records of phone calls during the Nixon administration. There are many instances where Nixon used Positive Inducement to attempt to either sway or maintain the support of members of Congress. The following is a brief description of phone calls associated with two such instances.

In the spring of 1969, the House of Representatives approved an extension of Elementary and Secondary Education Act programs through 1972 (The Senate approved this extension early the following year, and it was signed into law by Nixon that spring). Just prior to the scheduled vote on the extension however, there was an amendment offered:

> The major vote came just before passage, when a coalition of 227 Republicans and Southern Democrats helped adopt, by a 235-184 roll-call vote, an amendment offered by Rep. Edith Green (D Ore.) rewriting the entire bill. The major change between the Green bill and the one reported by the Education and Labor Committee (H Rept 91-114) was the two-year extension sought by Nixon Administration rather than a five-year continuation favored by a majority of Committee members . . .

> Mrs. Green, second ranking Committee Democrat, was joined by William H. Ayres (R Ohio) and Albert H. Quie (R Minn.), the first and second ranking Republicans on the Committee, Phil M. Landrum (D Ga.) and Robert N. Giaimo (D Conn.) in sponsoring the successful version of the bill . . . (HOUSE EXTENDS 1969).

This is the same Representative Green that was the subject of Negative Inducement by the Johnson Administration some years earlier, as noted above! This time, however, with a different president in the White House, instead of punishment, she received the reward of a personal congratulatory phone call, as did Republican Representatives Ayres and Quie, and Minority Whip Leslie Arends (R-IL). On April 23rd, 1969, shortly after the vote, the President phoned Rep. Arends at 1:23pm and spoke for approximately 2 minutes. He then called Rep. Green at 1:32pm and spoke for approximately 3 minutes. He spoke to Rep. Ayres for about a minute at 1:36pm, and to Rep. Quie for about 4 minutes at 1:38pm. All of these calls are noted in the Daily Diary and the first box of the President's Office Files (POF 1, found at the Nixon Project of the National Archives) as being congratulatory calls. Earlier that day, at 1:16pm, Nixon attempted to call House Minority Leader Gerald Ford (R-MI), presumably to offer similar congratulations, but Rep. Ford could not be reached at the time. The next day, at 2:43pm, Nixon successfully reached Rep. Ford and offered his congratulations in an approximately 11 minute phone call. A similar congratulatory call was placed to Rep. Joe Waggoner (D-LA) for his support in helping to shape the final bill. His wife took the call in his absence (Even though this call did not reach Rep. Waggoner directly, it was still coded as a Negative Inducement since it is reasonable to presume that Rep. Waggoner got the message!).

In the spring of 1970, Nixon's nominee to the Supreme Court, Harold Carswell, faced a difficult (and ultimately unsuccessful) time in Senate. On April 6th, 1970, a vote to send the nomination back to the Judiciary Committee for further hearings — essentially an attempt to bury the nomination — was defeated on the Senate floor by a vote of 44-52 (SENATE REJECTS 1970). Immediately after the vote, Nixon phoned Senator John S. Cooper (R-Ky) and spoke to him for three minutes (from 2:05pm to 2:08pm) to thank him for his help in defeating the Carswell recommittal vote. The call is listed in the Daily Diary for that day, and the topic is noted in Bob Haldeman's notes (Haldeman Box 139 at the Nixon Project). The next day, during a meeting with Senator Robert Dole, President Nixon placed a similar phone call to Senator Robert Griffin (R-Mi.). This call is also described in Haldeman's notes of the meeting (Haldeman Box 139 at the Nixon Project), and is found in the Daily Diary as having occurred at 6:19pm, a little over half an hour into the meeting. The call to Senator Cooper is coded as three minutes of positive inducement and the call to Senator Griffin was coded as one minute of Positive Inducement, as the president spoke only briefly before turning the call over to Senator Dole.

Organization

Recall that, as defined in Chapter 3, *Organization* is a strategic behavior that involves setting up rules and procedures, whether *ad hoc* or standard, with the goal of increasing the likelihood that the president's program, or any piece of presidentially-based legislation will be passed by Congress.

On the second page of Figure 5-3 (below), there are directions from President Nixon that are consistent with this definition:

RN suggested a meeting with Southern Senators and Congressmen. "To the extent we can stop this poisonous thing from happening" (bussing)[sic] the President states, "we ought to do it." . . .

Further, on legislation, the President recommended that the Congressmen and Senators, back home, lay the groundwork for a Do-Nothing Congress charge.

These selections were coded as a total of five lines of Organizational Behavior. Given the meeting length of 116 minutes, as noted in the Daily Diary (the meeting began at 8:05am and ended at 10:01am on March 28th, 1972), and the approximately 45-line length of the memo, that works out to around 13 minutes of Organizational Behavior.

Figure 5-3: Memo By Patrick Buchanan On A Republican Congressional Leadership Meeting With President Nixon

THE WHITE HOUSE

WASHINGTON
March 28, 1972

MEMORANDUM FOR THE PRESIDENT'S FILES

FROM: PATRICK J. BUCHANAN

SUBJECT: GOP Leadership Meeting, March 28, 1972

The morning meeting consisted of briefings and discussions on
a) bussing and the progress of the President' s program on the
Hill and b) the state of the economy.

Richardson led off saying that never in fifteen years of testifying
up on the Hill had he run into the kind of opposition he did on the
President's bussing proposals. He felt like the Indians were
circling and one knew not from which direction they would attack.

MacGregor briefed on the status of the President's legislation for
an extended period of time (This was prior to a Congressional
holiday); and the outlook can be described as anywhere from dubious
to grim.

Dominick indicated RN's compensatory education program could
come out of Congress with $2. 5 to $5 billion attached. If the
"concept survives, there will be a big price tag on it."

Poff indicated that in White House briefing memoranda, more
reference should be made to Article III of the Constitution; and
urged that we deal with the question of the power to re-open those
court decrees affecting the South. We are having trouble selling
this to the Southern contingent, Poff noted; and he stated, "some
of our Southerners feel they are about to be snookered" -- with
the moratorium for the North on bussing coming now, and relief
for the South, after the election.

The President stepped in to ask, "Does anyone here believe we
could get a Constitutional amendment through the Senate this year?"
None responded affirmatively.

- 2-

As for the moratorium, Poff said that it could not get out of Cellar' s Judiciary Committee -- and only a discharge petition could get out a modified version. "I am confident we cannot get a moratorium" out of Judiciary, he stated.

Griffin said he did not believe that "we can get a moratorium out of that conference, " (House-Senate higher education conference)

Ford indicated that we had a problem, a political problem, if we find something that protects the North and leaves the South under Court order.

RN suggested a meeting with Southern Senators and Congressmen. "To the extent we can stop this poisonous thing from happening "(bussing) the President states, "we ought to do it." Speaking of the judges, RN pointed to Griffin, "That jackass in your state," that "was political," that "fellow down there in Richmond," that was political. The implication was clear that the President felt that the judges watched the election returns.

Further, on legislation, the President recommended that the Congressmen and Senators, back home, lay the groundwork for a Do-Nothing Congress charge.

As for a "rump session" after the Conventions, the President said, "They're going to get one; September is a nice month to be in Washington."

Dole indicated that he did not think the President' s legislation would do that much for him, "If you don't pass them, I think it will be better politically."

Stein then spoke on the Economy, with customary dryness and humor -- - providing statistics to the Congressmen and Senators to use in their return to the home districts.

Buchanan

Nixon often appears to be quite the organizational strategist as many of the records of his administration contain examples of Organizational activities. Below is another example of a passage from some meeting notes that was coded as Organizational Behavior. It comes from an April 7th 1970 memo from Legislative Liaison Bryce Harlow on a meeting between Nixon and Senator Robert Dole (R-KS) which lasted from 5:43pm to 6:38pm:

> The President talked of using Senators Cook, Dole and Baker (maybe also Packwood) as an organized group to handle fights in the Senate. The President stressed the necessity for such a group in view of the serious inadequacy of the present Republican leadership of the Senate.

Although the two main topics of this meeting were the pending nomination of Harold Carswell to the Supreme Court and the possible nomination of George Stafford among others to chair the Interstate Commerce Commission, this discussion of how to "handle fights in the Senate" preceded any substantive discussion (at least in the memo). As such, it is unclear whether this meant to apply specifically to presidential nominees or a broader purpose. Either way, the goal is clearly the furtherance of the president's goals in the Senate, and was coded as five lines — which worked out to approximately five minutes — of Organizational Activity.

Emphasis

As noted in Chapter 3, *Emphasis* Activities are strategic behaviors which involve the ordering of proposals submitted to Congress, the timing of such presentations, and how much they are stressed or mentioned.

Figure 5-4 is a segment from a memo that records a meeting between President Johnson and the Democratic Congressional Leadership on February 6th, 1968. This meeting began at 8:30am and lasted for two hours, until 10:31am[11]. On page 5 of the memo (below), under the heading of "Authorizations and Appropriations", the president asks if the Leadership "can help us accelerate this schedule or at the minimum hold to it — so that all appropriation bills are finally passed by June 30?" As this seems to fit the definition, it was coded as two lines of Emphasis Activity. Further down,

---

[11] The header on the memo claims that the meeting broke up at 9:25 am, but this is misleading. There were two parts to this meeting. The first part consisted of a discussion of military intelligence in general, and the VietNam war in particular. Most of this segment consisted of a dialogue between President Johnson and Senator Robert Byrd, who complained of intelligence failures. The president's participation in this segment, which ended at 9:25 am, was coded as Foreign Policy Activity. The second part of the meeting, which lasted from 9:25 am until 10:31 am, covers a wider variety of topics and is reprinted here.

under the heading of "Gold Cover", there are additional items coded as Emphasis Activity. Specifically, the sentence where the president asks "to have the bill considered by Rules as soon as the House returns February 19...", and the next line, "This is a very urgent item." These were coded as two and one half lines of Emphasis Activity. Given that the section of the memo reprinted below is approximately 40 lines in length, and represents about 66 minutes of time, the segments coded as Emphasis Activity total approximately 7 minutes in length.

Figure 5-4: Segment Of Notes From A Democratic Congressional Leadership Meeting With President Johnson, February 6, 1968

The following is the agenda discussed:

Message Scheduling

The Education Message went Monday. Tentatively, the Consumer Message is slated for Tuesday, the Crime Message for Wednesday, and the Foreign Aid Message for Thursday.

Joe Califano will have the most recent schedule in the event you with to confirm these dates and dates of messages beyond this week.

The House will be out of session from the time it adjourns this week until Monday, February 19. The Senate will reconvene Wednesday, February 14. If you want to send any messages next week the House will have a pro forma session Thursday, February 15. But if you propose to send any messages next week I suggest you mention the possibility to the leadership.

- 5 -

This week's schedule:

House: Export-Import Bank
  Fire Research and Safety

Senate: Civil Rights Debate

Passage of the Export-Import Bank bill seems assured. We are supporting
the committee bill even though it has two bad features. We need to fight
off further damaging amendments and we will need the leadership's help
with the conferees, as the bill must go to conference.

Fire Research and Safety is a holdover from last week. It is a consumer
bill and we hope to obtain final passage this week.

On the Civil Rights legislation we would hope that the Senate Leadership is looking
toward a compromise or cloture. You may wish to sound them out
on the current floor situation.

Authorizations and Appropriations

I am attaching a list provided to us by the departments of the dates set for
commencing hearings on authorization and appropriation measures.

Can the Leadership help us accelerate this schedule or at the minimum hold
to it - so that all appropriation bills are finally passed by June 30?

Rules Committee

Pending in Rules Committee are the following major Administration measures:

  Arts and Humanities Foundation
  Jury Reform
  Highway Beautification
  D.C. Constitutional Amendment

The Leadership has asked Colmer to have special meetings of Rules
to consider rules on the first two.

The Highway Beautification bill will be tough on the floor. Should we consider further
reducing the authorization in the bill in an effort to gain support? Sometime we are going
to have to get a rule on this bill and face up to it on the floor.

- 6 -

D.C. Constitutional Amendment is another tough one. We should decide
soon whether to hold it in Rules pending Senate action, or whether to abandon
it for this session and try to move the bill which would provide D.C. with a
non-voting Representative in the House.

Perhaps the Senate Leadership could give us a reading on prospects for moving the
Constitutional Amendment out of Senate Judiciary where it
presently languishes.

Gold Cover

We hope for Senate passage this week.

In the House we would like to have the bill considered by Rules as soon as
the House returns February 19, so that the bill can be finally passed that
week.

This is a very urgent item.

D.C. Elected School Board

We hope that the Leadership can get the conferees together soon so that this
bill can be enacted. It means a lot in the District of Columbia and its
enactment will be a plus for the Administration.

Chapter 6: Considerations of Validity and Reliability

Each president leaves behind a legacy and a legend. Each leaves reality and myth. These are usually the result of a myriad of observations made by staffers, assistants, observers, and confidantes over the course of an administration. As such, even the myths are usually grounded in *some* reality. Presidents are boiled down to a handful of catch phrases. Nowhere is this is more true than with presidents Eisenhower, Johnson, and Nixon. The ability to capture — and *consistently* capture — aspects of their legends provides some evidence of the validity and reliability of the approach used this project.

Some Initial Notes on the Samples

Chapter 4 briefly noted the periods of time from which the dataset for this project is drawn. To recap, it covers the four-month periods from January 20th through May 19th of 1953, 1954, 1956, 1965, 1966, 1968, 1969, 1970, and 1972. It is not a random sample of activities, days, months, or years. There are reasons for this lack of randomness. The rationale for selecting the years was laid out in footnote 8 on page 21 (in Chapter 4). The rationale for having contiguous four-month periods of time sampled within these years instead of random samples is mainly a pragmatic one: feasibility. Gathering the data is an extremely labor-intensive, time consuming process. The records in each presidential library are still almost exclusively on paper. This research requires translating presidential diary entries into machine-readable data. Given the available methods and resources of the time the sample was gathered, it required a total of six months of eight-hour day six-day weeks. The contiguous sample required examining and coding the diaries and related materials for one-quarter of each of the sample years. A truly random sample of days would have greatly increased the time it took to gather the data because it would have required examining samples from a much greater range of each of the sample years. However, even though the sample is not random, it does capture a fair range of variation in each president's time in office.

This can be illustrated by examining the sample periods using recorded presidential approval ratings as a set of markers for each administration. While the samples are not perfect mirrors of each presidency (again, as defined by approval ratings), the samples do seem to capture a fair amount of the variety of approval ratings for each president. This is evident from examining figures 6-1, 6-2, and 6-3. The Eisenhower sample captures approval ratings from 61% to 77%. This captures most of the range of his entire time in office (48% to 79%), and covers virtually the entire range of his first term — from which the sample was drawn (57% to 77%). The Johnson sample captures approval ratings from 41% to 71%. This also captures most of the range of his entire time in office (35% to 80%), and covers most of the range of his only full term — from which the sample was drawn (35% to 71%). The Nixon sample captures approval ratings from 50% to 65%. This captures only part of the range of his entire time in office (23% to 67%), but covers the range of his first term quite well (48% to 67%). The range of approval ratings for Eisenhower and Johnson are captured fairly well, while Nixon is less well covered. What is missing from their times in office can best be described by noting the major events of the times not included in the sample. There appears to be one major missing period of time in each administration. In the Eisenhower administration, the data do not capture the recession of 1958. In the Johnson administration, the data do not capture the post-Kennedy assassination period of 1964 — most notably the time of the passage of the Civil Rights Act of 1964. Finally, and perhaps most notably, the Nixon data do not capture any of the Watergate scandal.

So, the data do miss some notable periods of time in each administration. However, given the circumstances necessitating its gatherance as such, the data do cover a good range (defined at least, by approval ratings) of each administration.

The next thing to explore is whether or not the data as gathered can not only discover things not known about these presidents, but also whether or not they can confirm what *is* known about them. This kind of confirmation is the best evidence of the usefullness of the data.

Figure 6-1: Eisenhower Approval Ratings, 1953-1956

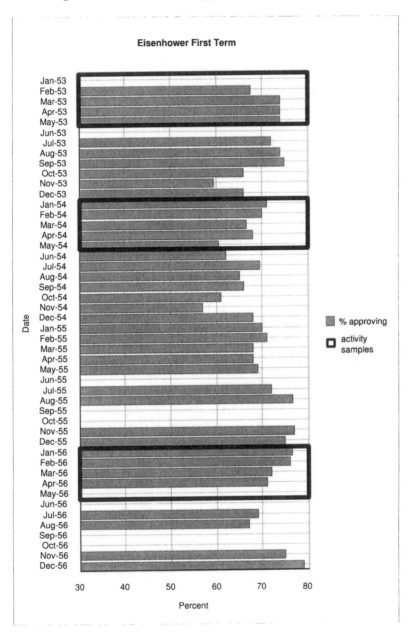

Source: Lyn Ragsdale, *Vital Statistics on the Presidency* (Washington, D.C.: Congressional Quarterly Press, 1998), 129-30.

Figure 6-2: Johnson Approval Ratings, 1965-1969

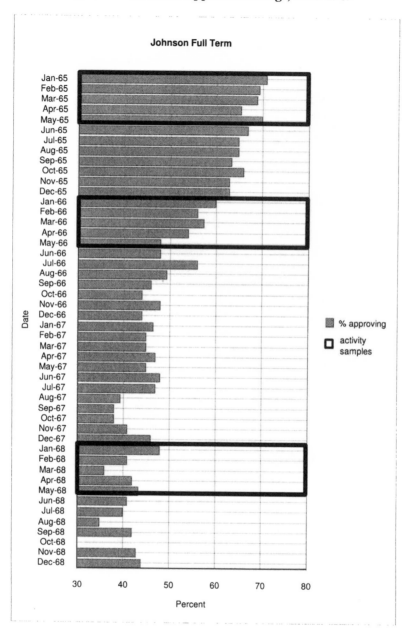

Johnson Full Term

Source: Lyn Ragsdale, *Vital Statistics on the Presidency* (Washington, D.C.: Congressional Quarterly Press, 1998), 129-30.

Figure 6-3: Nixon Approval Ratings, 1969-1974

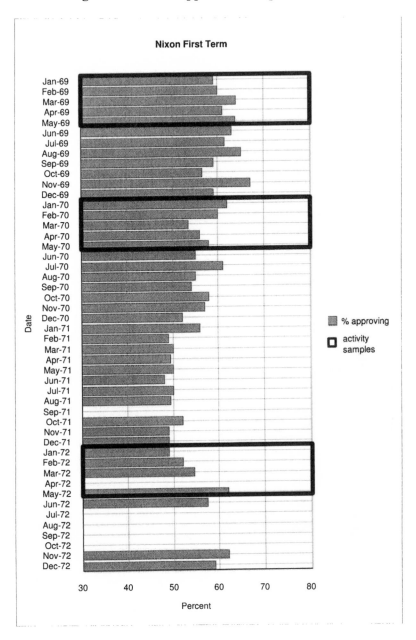

Source: Lyn Ragsdale, *Vital Statistics on the Presidency* (Washington, D.C.:
Congressional Quarterly Press, 1998), 129-30.

For instance, the levels of energy and activity associated with these presidents are major components of their enduring personae. This is no more evident than in James David Barber's (1985) categorizations of presidential character. On his active-passive dimension, he places Eisenhower squarely on the passive side. Conversely, he uses both Johnson and Nixon as proto-typically active presidents.

His discussion of Eisenhower clearly is of a president who simply doesn't do — and doesn't want to do — very much:

> On a great many occasions in the biographies Eisenhower is found asserting himself by denying himself, taking a strong stand against the suggestion that he take a strong stand. . . .

> His character is further illuminated in his complaints, which are concentrated around the theme of being bothered. His temper flared when he felt he was being imposed upon, interfered with on matters that he wanted others to handle. . . .

> "He once told the Cabinet," [Sherman] Adams reports, "that if he was able to do nothing as President except balance the budget he would feel that his time in the White House had been well spent." (Barber 1985)

Barber is not the only one who sees Eisenhower in this light. According to Fred Greenstein (1982), the traditional view of Eisenhower is that of "an aging hero who reigned more than he ruled and who lacked the energy, motivation, and political skill to have a significant impact on events." Even Greenstein's 'revisionist view' of Eisenhower stresses effectiveness based on the "hidden-hand" *quality* of his actions as opposed to any sizeable *quantity* of activity. The delegation of authority was a centerpiece of Eisenhower's administrative style (Anderson 1968; Polsby 1986). His purpose in delegating as much authority as possible was to remove himself from the day-to-day minutiae of the executive branch. His interest was in the overall picture, not the details.

By contrast Lyndon Johnson is never described as anything but a whirlwind of activity. "His fantastic pace of action in the Presidency was obvious", Barber (1985) says. He quotes Johnson as saying "Every job I've had is bigger than I am, and I have to work twice as hard as the next man to do it." (Barber 1985)

Doris Kearns (1976) indicates that, upon ascending to the presidency, Johnson's energy level seemed redoubled. He talked with chiefs of state; sent messages to Congress; issued orders to the executive branch; met with businessmen, labor leaders, and civil servants. The hours between 2 and 6 a.m. were all that Johnson grudgingly gave to sleep. . . . His mind remained resilient even when his body was fatigued. He tended to rest from one kind of activity by engaging in another.

She further notes:

In the first two years of his presidency Johnson seemed to be everywhere — calling for new programs and for action on the old, personally organizing his shifting congressional majorities, signing bills, greeting tourists, settling labor disputes, championing the blacks, constantly on the telephone to publishers, businessmen, astronauts, farm leaders, in a working day that began at 7 a.m. when he watched simultaneously, the morning shows of all three networks and that ended sometime in the early hours of the next morning.

In the same vein, Barber describes Nixon as a very active president as well. He describes Nixon as having

poured on energy, day and night, at home and away. His Presidential activities came to take up nearly all his waking hours . . .

Others also talk of Nixon in this manner. Stephen Ambrose (1992) refers to him as "a man whose mind was always leaping into the future." Bruce Mazlish (1972) notes:

Outstanding among them [the various "sides" of Nixon] is what I shall call Nixon's fear of passivity. He is afraid of being acted upon, of being inactive, of being soft, of being thought impotent, and of being dependent on any one else.

Garry Wills (1970) discusses Nixon's own views on his activity. In interviewing him, Wills noted his many referrals to Theodore Roosevelt and asked

if he felt any special affinity to the Republican Roosevelt. "Not so much in ideas." . . . "I guess I'm like him in one way only: I like to be in the arena. I have seen those who have nothing to do — I could be one of them if I wanted — the people just lying around at Palm Beach. Nothing could be more pitiful." His voice had contempt in it, not pity.

Elizabeth Drew (1976) describes Nixon in a manner similar to Kearns description of Johnson. She claims Nixon desired to work "16 to 18" hours a day.

Given these characterizations, one expects most measures of activity to attribute a higher level to Johnson and Nixon than to Eisenhower. However, none of the above observations are based on any systematic measurements. Fortunately, the activity data is able to dramatically confirm this expectation. During the periods sampled for this project, Eisenhower initiates approximately 16 distinct activities per day. By stark contrast, Nixon initiates about 38 and Johnson initiates over 66 distinct activities per day. Figure 6-4 graphically demonstrates that at every hour of the day, Johnson and Nixon average a notably greater number of activities initiated than does Eisenhower.

It is clear from the data that both Johnson and Nixon initiated more activities than Eisenhower during an average day. What is not clear from the above is what kind of activities they initiated. Not all activities are necessarily evidence of great energy. For instance, another thing Kearns notes in her biography is that Johnson had a particular knack for taking "cat-naps" at almost any time during the day. These are included in the totals in Figure 6-4, but it is unfair and misleading, to use these "activities" as evidence of one's energy!

Since, as noted earlier, each observation is coded for the type of activity, a rough grouping can be created from the data to examine the distinction between "working" and "non-working" activities. This may be achieved by grouping activities coded as Executive, Foreign Policy/Diplomatic, and Legislative in the "working" category, and by grouping Personal and Social/Ceremonial activities into the "non-working" category. The duration of activities can then be totaled for each category. Table 6-1 reveals that each day, Nixon and Johnson spend approximately 40% of their days "working", but Eisenhower spends only about 20% of his day "working". Given this, Johnson and Nixon clearly appear to be the more active presidents.

Figure 6-4 makes apparent more than just their respective levels of activity. The "shape" of their days differ as well. It looks as though Eisenhower springs to life after 7 a.m. and peaks at 9 a.m. His level of activity gradually fades throughout the remainder of the day. In contrast, Johnson's day is shaped quite differently. His activity peaks a bit later, at 11 a.m., and then peaks once again at 5 p.m. Unlike Eisenhower, Johnson's activities run well into the night, decreasing only after midnight (recall the Kearns quote on sleep above). There is also a notable decline in the middle of his day. This undoubtedly due in large part to the fact that he regularly took mid-afternoon naps. Robert Dallek describes this 'bi-modal' day in a book on Johnson:

Figure 6-4: Average Number of Activities Initiated per Hour

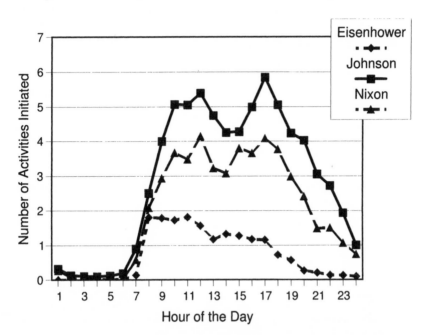

His agenda was so ambitious he needed a "two-shift day" to achieve it. Rising at 6:30 or 7:00 each morning, he began his workday in bed, where he read newspapers, the *Congressional Record*, and documents prepared by aides who conducted early morning business in the bedroom. Johnson thought nothing of placing early morning phone calls to congressmen and senators. . . . Reaching the Oval Office at about nine, Johnson worked until 2 p.m., when he exercised by vigorously walking around the White House grounds or taking a swim.

The second half of his "day" started at 4 p.m. After a nap in his pajamas, a shower, and fresh clothes. It lasted until at least midnight and often until one or two o'clock in the morning (Dallek 1998).

This "two-shift day" appears quite obvious in Johnson's Daily Diaries. It readily shows up in the data.

Like Eisenhower, Nixon is up by 7 a.m. He maintains a fairly constant level of activity throughout the day. This level drops around 6 or 7 p.m. However, like Johnson, he is usually active well into the night. Table 6-1 gives us an idea of the different activity levels of the three presidents, and Figure 6-4 (above) shows us the different distributions of activity throughout their days:

Table 6-1: Minutes Per Day Spent By Type Of Activity (Workday)

	Leg. Acts	Leg. Contacts[a]	Executive	Foreign Policy	Workday[b]
Eisenhower	5.4	29.6	175.6	61	271.6
Johnson	11.1	37	325.2	112.6	485.9
Nixon	7.7	23.6	296.5	124.1	451.8

[a]Leg. Contacts are all contacts with members of Congress or the Liaison staff not otherwise coded.
[b]Calculated as the sum of Leg. Acts, Leg. Contact, Executive, and Foreign Policy

Table 6-1 (continued): Minutes Per Day Spent By Type Of Activity (Social & Personal)

	Social	Personal	Total[c]
Eisenhower	283.7	886.3	1441.5
Johnson	257.1	701.6	1444.7
Nixon	149.3	839.8	1440.9

[c]Calculated as the sum of Workday, Social, and Personal. Totals may vary due to rounding, coding peculiarities, and random error (a 24-hour day is 1440 minutes).

The benefit of the data is that they are useful not only to quantify the overall descriptions of an administration, but also more specific assertions. For instance, it has been noted that Johnson's penchant for using the telephone was legendary whereas Eisenhower actually disliked using it. Little, if anything, has been said of Nixon's phone use specifically, but some speculations are possible. I will address them shortly. Johnson's use of the phone is nowhere better indicated than in several quotes from Merle Miller's biography (1980):

> William Jorden: "He [Johnson] was an inveterate user of Alexander Graham Bell's instrument and it didn't take very much to prompt him to pick up. . . . I think it was the thing that almost did him in . . . trying to talk over two or three telephones at the same time."

> Robert C. Weaver: "I think he would have called Jesus Christ on the telephone if he had a number for Him, at any time. . . ."

This is also discussed by Barber (1985): "He was in a constant whirl of conversation, face to face and on the telephone." By contrast, Sherman Adams (1962) says that

> [b]ecause Eisenhower disliked talking business on the phone, [Wilton] Persons and I and a few other staff members would speak for him on the telephone on many matters that required his personal attention.

These impressions are indeed are borne out in the data. Figure 6-5 shows that, as with overall activity, Johnson was much more likely than Eisenhower to initiate a phone call at most any time of the day. The only time they ever display comparable levels are the hours of 2 to 6 a.m., which Kearns is quoted earlier as saying were "grudgingly [given by Johnson] to sleep."

The contrast is equally striking when one examines the average amount of time spent on the phone each day. Table 6-2 presents these amounts for the Eisenhower, Johnson, and Nixon samples. Eisenhower spent less than 40 minutes on the phone on an average day, initiating less than ½ hour of those calls. Nixon spent just over an hour, initiating most all of those. But Johnson spent a staggering 3½ hours on the phone each day, and over 2 hours of that placing calls — at almost any hour of the day! A not-atypical event:

> "I hope I didn't wake ya," LBJ told Ohio Congressman Wayne Hayes one morning at 6 a.m. "Oh no," Hayes replied. "I was lying here just hoping you would call." (Dallek 1998)

Of Nixon's phone use, one can only speculate. If anything, little has been written of it. The average daily time he spent on the phone is a bit more than Eisenhower (and only about one third that of Johnson), but as Figure 6-5 shows, he handled approximately twice as many phone calls at any given time.

Table 6-2: Minutes Per Day Spent On The Telephone

	Outgoing[a]	Incoming	Total
Eisenhower	27.8	10.9	38.7
Johnson	132.1	70.4	202.5
Nixon	64.3	6.4	70.7

[a]All figures in minutes per day.

Lyndon Johnson's Phone Console (Yoichi Okamoto, LBJ Library)

If anything stands out, it is the disparity of time spent on outgoing as compared to incoming calls apparent in Table 6-2. It is on the order of ten to one. One explanation that fits well with this observation is his well-documented need for control. Barber and many others speak of this (e.g.: see Wills 1970; Mazlish 1972). Mazlish (1972) speaks of Nixon's "anality" as manifested by "his intense need for control: control of himself, control of others, and control of the world around him." A discussion of phone use in connection with this can reasonably revolve around someone using it mostly to call people up and tell them what to do.

Figure 6-5: Average Number of Phonecalls per Hour

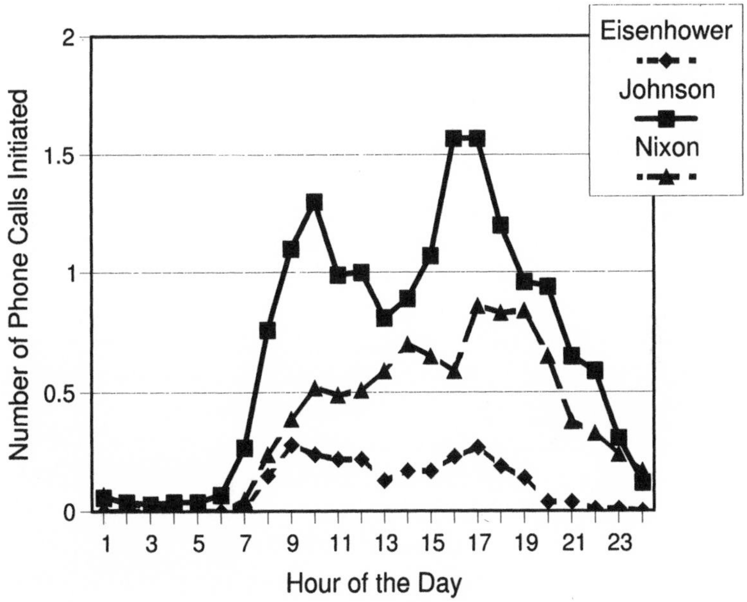

Another assertion which is verifiable via the data involves Nixon's travel schedule. The general belief is that he spent notably more time away from the White House than other presidents. Of Nixon's travel, Barber (1985) says,

He was a man in motion, relentlessly flying off to Camp David, Key Biscayne, or San Clemente . . .

Theodore White (1975) makes the point a bit more systematically by noting that by November 1973, Nixon had stayed in Washington D.C. for only four of forty-four weekends in his second term.

By coding each activity for its location, these assertions are easily verifiable. When searching the Location variable for activities occurring outside the White House, it turns out that Nixon spent almost twice as much time traveling as did the others. Eisenhower spent 12% of his time away from the White House, Johnson — 10%, and Nixon almost 20%.

Returning to Eisenhower, another verifiable assertion involves what Greenstein (1982) calls much publicized "periodic dampers" inserted into Eisenhower's schedule. Concern for the health of one of the oldest people ever to attain the office lead Eisenhower's doctors to deliberately work in regularly scheduled breaks into his schedule. Again, we can turn to the Location coding for help. It turns out that Eisenhower traveled to Burning Tree Country Club to play golf 18 times in the 120 day sample of 1953. That averages out to almost exactly once a week. The usual sequence involved heading out to Burning Tree around noon, and spending the rest of the day there.

The data presented so far, when viewed in light of the descriptive accounts of Eisenhower, Johnson, and Nixon pulled from the literature, speak well of the reliability and validity of the approach. They produce quantitative confirmation of descriptive accounts of these presidents. The various codings clearly and consistently reflect the "desired construct[s]" (Judd 1991). Proceeding further into the intended exploration and analysis can apparently be pursued with a fair degree of confidence.

The following chapters do just that. The first subject is the investigation into the many aspects of presidential activity in general. Next, the more specific issue of contact with members of Congress is addressed. Here, a second dataset, focusing specifically on congressional contact is developed. In this section, presidential activities are explored, not only as a dependent variable, but also as an independent variable — addressing the possibility that contact plays some part in the success or failure of an administration.

Chapter 7: Results I

The purpose of this research is to explore a way to more fully and accurately assess presidential influence in the legislative arena. As noted in Chapter 2, the existing studies of influence are geared more towards measures of *success* and not true influence. Measures of true influence require knowing what the president is actually doing to further his legislative proposals.

The chapters subsequent to Chapter 2 described and examined a dataset of presidential activity collected for a sample of modern presidents. The question remains: can this data actually be used to *learn* about presidential behavior? More importantly, can this research move beyond the notion of uniqueness often ascribed to the behavior of each administration toward examining behaviors common across administrations?

What follows is an examination of presidential behavior that conforms closely to criteria for research set forth at the beginning of this project. While some scholars are already moving in this more analytical direction (e.g., Lewis and Strine 1996), the data tends to be more demographic and situational than behavioral. The presidential dataset described in previous chapters is used to address several hypotheses about presidential behavior — specifically, presidential behavior in the legislative arena.

Organization Over Time

On January 21, 1953, shortly after 7:30 A.M., I entered the oval room of the West Wing of the White House . . . .
At two minutes after eight I had my first official conference as President, with Herbert Brownell, the Attorney General-designate. We

discussed matters that had absorbed our attention for the weeks just past: appointments, nominations to office, Senate confirmation of appointees, and conflict-of-interest laws.

-Dwight D. Eisenhower
Mandate for Change, 1953-1956

The first task of any new president is to organize. The primacy of organizing is an inevitable result of our system of separated powers. Presidential scholars often point to Richard Neustadt's (1990) famous observation that ours is "a government of separated institutions *sharing* powers". In such a system, as Neustadt also observes, "[t]he President ha[s] no power . . . to gain his ends by fiat" and must resort to persuasion to achieve his goals (Neustadt 1990). This leads Charles O. Jones to say that "it is a fair restatement of Neustadt's sage observation to say that we have a government of separated institutions *competing* for shared powers" (Jones 1995, emphasis added; see also Pious 1996)[12].

There is ample evidence that this necessity to organize vis-a-vis Congress is not lost on incoming presidents. Witness these statements by Dwight Eisenhower and Lyndon Johnson, respectively:

In setting up this organization [the White House Staff], one of the most important functions was that of maintaining liaison between the President and members of the Congress (Eisenhower 1963).

Every President has to establish with the various sectors of the country what I call "the right to govern." . . . Every President has to become a leader, and to be a leader he must attract people who are willing to follow him. . . . Under our system of government, with its clearly defined separation of powers, the greatest threat to the Chief Executive's "right to govern" comes traditionally from the Congress (Johnson 1971).

These quotes recount what was on the minds of Eisenhower and Johnson upon their taking office. Organizing is clearly prominent in their thoughts. The first testable hypothesis about presidential behavior in the legislative arena then explores the extent to which they act on these thoughts:

---

[12] This reflects, at least in part, a conscious decision on the part of the Framers of the Constitution. In *Federalist* 51, James Madison advocates "giving to those who administer each department the necessary constitutional means and personal motives to resist encroachments of the others . . . . Ambition must be made to counteract ambition".

H1. **Organizational activity should be a greater percentage of overall legislative activity at the beginning of an administration than at any other time.**

Recall from the chapter 3 that activities coded as *Organizational* involve creating rules and procedures whose goal is to increase the likelihood that any piece of the president's program will pass Congress. Staffing, rule-making, and any practices set up for interacting with Congress are considered *organizational activities* to the extent that their objective is the creation of future leverage.

To investigate H1, the first thing to do is to calculate the total amount of time spent (in minutes) coded broadly as legislative activities. The totals, a compilation of data for all three presidents, appear in Table 7-1 below. *Year* refers to the year after initial election (e.g., Year 1 for Eisenhower is 1953, for Johnson is 1965, and for Nixon is 1969). In this particular table, Σ *leg* is the number of minutes spent in activities coded as legislative. So, for the first year samples of these administrations, the three presidents engaged in a total of 701 minutes of identifiably legislative activities. In the second year samples they logged 1523 minutes; and in the fourth year samples they logged 1942 minutes (data was not collected for the third years). It is clear that these presidents engaged in much *more* legislative activities *of all types* after their first years in office.

Table 7-1: Time Spent In Legislative Activities Per Year

Year	Σ leg
1	701
2	1523
3	na
4	1942
Totals	4166

In order to find the percentage of legislative activities which are organizational in nature, the next step is to identify *organizational activities* according to the above description. The database of activities yields the totals shown in Table 7-2. Σ *org* is the number of minutes spent in activities coded as *organizational* according to the above description. So, for the first years of their administrations, the three presidents engaged in a total of 277 minutes of legislative activity that was coded as *organizational* legislative activities. In their second years, they logged 486 minutes, and in their fourth years they logged 458 minutes.

Table 7-2: Time Spent In Organizing Per Year

Year	Σ org
1	277
2	486
3	na
4	458
Totals	1221

Combining the Organizational and Legislative data shows how much Legislative time was spent specifically in Organizational activities for each year. The totals are shown below in Table 7-3. *%Org* is the percentage of all *legislative* activities coded as *organizational* (Σ Organizing/Σ Legislative). So, for example, of the 701 minutes the three presidents spent in legislative activities during their combined first years in office, 277 minutes were coded as *organizational* legislative activities. Thus, 39.5% of all legislative activities in the first years were organizational. Consistent with H1, we can see that this percentage *drops* in the second year to 31.9% and to just 23.6% by the fourth year.

Table 7-3: Time Spent In Organizing Per Year As A Percentage Of All Legislative Activities

Year	Σ Organizing	Σ Legislative	%Org (org/leg)
1	277	701	39.5%
2	486	1523	31.9%
3	na	na	na
4	458	1942	23.6%
Totals	1221	4166	29.3%

Significant Differences?

In testing for significance, each minute of activity is used as an individual case. Thus, the percentage of organizational activities is also the probability that any individual minute is one of organizational activity. In other words, since in year one 39.5% of all legislative activities are organizational in nature, it can be said that there is a 39.5% chance that any individual minute is organizational in nature, *or* that the typical organizational "score" for any given period of legislative activity is .395. So, using these as means, we can calculate the standardized distances between each combination of years (z-score). In comparing years 1 and 2, we find a z-score of 3.5; in comparing years 2 and 4, we find a z-score of 5.5; and in comparing years 1 and 4, we find a z-score of 8.0. That is, the mean for year two is 3.5 standard deviations from the mean for year one; the mean for year four is 5.5 standard deviations from the mean for year two; and the mean for year four is eight standard deviations from the mean for year one. These constitute statistically significant differences from one year to the next ($a_{year1,year2} \leq 0.0002$, $a_{2,4} < 0.0001$, and $a_{1,4} < 0.0001$). It seems that, as presidents spend more and more time in the legislative arena, a diminishing percentage of that time is spent in organizational activities.

Strategy and Legislative Experience

For my part, I early embarked on a program of discussion issues, in a social atmosphere, with groups of congressmen and senators of both parties, in the hope that personal acquaintance would help smooth out difficulties inherent in partisanship. . . . I set up a staff section in the White House with the mission of maintaining effective liaison between the Congress and me . . .

But of all the mechanisms for developing coordination between the White House and the Congress — particularly with the Republican members — by far the most effective was the weekly meeting I held with the Legislative leaders.

-Dwight D. Eisenhower
Mandate for Change, 1953-1956

The most important factor that influenced my decision to press for congressional actions was this: if any sense were to come of the senseless events which had brought me to the Office of the Presidency, it would come only from my using the experience I had gained as a legislator to encourage the legislative process to function as the modern era required.

-Lyndon B. Johnson
The Vantage Point

The previous section discussed the importance of organization to any administration. The above quotes provide some insight into *how much* organization plays a part in various administrations. Eisenhower stresses organization as a primary form of interaction with Congress, whereas Johnson talks just as much about the need to "press for congressional actions" (i.e., *do* something) as he does about the need to "encourage the legislative process to function" (i.e., plan or strategize). "From the start of his presidency," Robert Dallek notes, "Johnson had focused on asserting his control over Congress as a prelude to getting major legislation." (Dallek 1998)

Organizational activities, along with Emphasis activities are part of those described in Chapter 3 as "Strategic" activities. The focus of such behavior is generally broad and long-term. Contrast this with the short-term, more individual-level activities previously termed "Pitches". An obvious distinction between these two types of activities is that Pitching requires much more personal familiarity and contact with the intended target. As such, one would expect presidents with knowledge of and familiarity with members of Congress to engage in more pitching activities, while presidents who are 'legislative novices' should feel more of the need to plan and organize — in other words, pursue strategic activities — as a prelude to pitching. So Eisenhower, coming from outside Washington D.C. and unfamiliar with many members of Congress, would feel more comfortable following the latter course, while consummate insider Johnson would be much more likely to pursue the former course. However, simply totaling the minutes spent by each president in strategic activities yields a misleading picture on the use of this type of activity since they devote widely differing amounts of time to legislative activities (see the fourth column in Table 7-4, below). In fact, a simple total *does* show that strategic activities increase with legislative experience. This is because legislative activity *overall* varies directly with legislative experience. So, the second testable hypothesis is best stated as follows:

H2. **The percentage of Strategic (Emphasis and Organization) activity and especially the subset of Organizational activity should vary inversely with a president's level of legislative experience.**

When the hypothesis is explored in this manner however, the results, shown in Table 7-4 below, appear mixed at best. It appears that Nixon — who's legislative experience falls somewhere between Eisenhower's and Johnson's — was the true strategist of the three. Seventy percent of all his identifiably Legislative activities were also identified as Strategic activities.

Johnson falls in the middle while Eisenhower appears to be the true "pitcher". This finding is actually closer to the *opposite* of the hypothesis! Curiously, if we break down the data by year in office, a pattern emerges. The hypothesis is actually *supported* by the first year data (see Figure 7-1, above). There is a small but statistically significant negative correlation (-.19, p<.05) between legislative experience and strategic activities, and a stronger significant negative correlation (-.30 p<.01) between legislative experience and organizational activities. The story that emerges from the first year data is of a congressionally inexperienced Eisenhower and Nixon essentially trying to figure it all out — focusing more on strategy and organization than the more experienced Johnson, who dives right into the "sell". Less congressionally experienced, and thus probably less comfortable with the "sell", Eisenhower and Nixon concentrate on the "grand strategy" (recall Eisenhower's comments, quoted at the beginning of this section). This is exemplified in the notes from one of Eisenhower's first cabinet meetings, on January 30, 1953:

> The President spoke about his own efforts to cultivate cooperative relations with Congress as a means of providing a firm basis for getting considered treatment and respect for Executive proposals. He presented his plan to have luncheons with all the committee chairmen of the House and of the Senate next week, with Vice President Nixon attending both luncheons in his executive capacity. The President commented on General Persons' remark about wedge-driving to the effect that if Cabinet Members are good friends, they can laugh off efforts made to divide them. The President believes the best approach in regard to asserted difficulties with Congress would be to maintain a silence "of confidence", for he expects any early difficulties to work themselves out if the fire is not fed (Minnich 1953).

Table 7-4: Strategic Activity As A Percentage Of Legislative Activity By Level Of Experience

President	Leg. Experience[a]	Σ Strategy	Σ Legislative	%Strategy (strat/leg)
Eisenhower	0	126	365	35%
Nixon	6	507	722	70%
Johnson	23.5	1243	3087	40%

[a]Total years in Congress plus ½ total as Vice President minus years out of government (minimum score of 0)

It is also exemplified in a January 28, 1969 meeting between Nixon and Republican congressional leaders in which approximately 40% of a two hour meeting is devoted to organizing policy task forces (President's Personal Files 1969 [PPF78]). However, while the hypothesis holds true for the first year, it does *not* hold for subsequent years, as Figure 7-1 illustrates. In year 1, H2 is clearly demonstrated. However, in years two and four, the percentage of strategic activity bears no connection at all to legislative experience. In fact, it seems that Eisenhower steadily becomes the engaged pitchman, Nixon becomes even more of an aloof strategist, and Johnson remains at an approximately constant middle-ground over time[13]. By Eisenhower's fourth year, he has clearly shifted over to pitching activities as the excerpts from notes on a February 28, 1956 meeting with congressional leaders demonstrate:

> Upper Colorado River Project — The President reaffirmed his previous statements on the importance of this project and requested all possible help toward approval of it. . . .

> National Security — The President reviewed the factors involved in the determination and provision of effective national security program (Minnich 1956).

As for Nixon, by his fourth year, strategic activity becomes even more common, as seen in a selection from the record of a March 28, 1972 meeting with Republican congressional leaders:

> Further, on legislation, the President recommended that the Congressmen and Senators, back home, lay the groundwork for a Do-Nothing Congress charge.

> As for a "rump session" after the Conventions, the President said, "They're going to get one; September is a nice month to be in Washington."

> [Senator Robert] Dole indicated that he did not think the President's legislation would do that much for him, "If you don't pass them, I think it will be better politically." (Buchanan 1972)

---

[13] It may be interesting to investigate Johnson's *true* first year in office — 1964 — to see if his level of strategic activity was any lower than in subsequent years. If the rationale presented here is correct, finding that LBJ's 1964 level of strategic activity is lower would be consistent with the idea that experience determines the first year, and after that, presidents level off at a level with which they are comfortable.

From the data, it appears that *new* presidents' behaviors are tempered by their experience, but immersion in the presidency rapidly overshadows previous experience. In other words, legislatively inexperienced presidents are *initially* more likely to resort to plotting strategy as opposed to pitching; but over time all presidents 'seek their own level' of strategic activity. After familiarizing himself with Congress, Eisenhower becomes more and more comfortable pitching, whereas the ever-mistrusting Nixon becomes ever more *un*comfortable with this type of activity and pulls further and further away from it, in favor of more and grander strategic activities (e.g., see Nathan 1975 and Light 1983).

Figure 7-1: Strategic Activity as a Percentage of All Legislative Activity

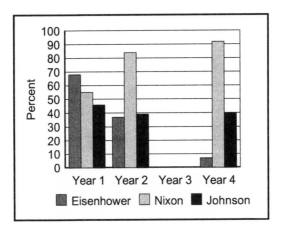

Cyclical Effects

> During his journey [to Asia], the President came up with the idea of a triumphal tour of the country to sign major Great Society bills Congress had passed. A whirlwind trip just before the November 8 [1966] election would highlight his accomplishments and give him a chance to help Democratic candidates for Congress and several statehouses.
> -Joseph A. Califano, Jr.
> *The Triumph and Tragedy of Lyndon Johnson*

Even though Johnson's planned "triumphal tour" never took place (Democrats fared poorly that year, and Johnson decided to avoid too close a connection with them), it highlights an important aspect of presidential behavior. Given the increasing value of public exposure and rhetoric to a president who is either up for re-election himself, or whose party is up for re-election, the calendar probably plays an important part in the activities presidents choose to pursue. In election years, they are more likely to pursue activities that highlight their (or their party's) accomplishments. There are few recorded instances where presidents are as deliberate as Johnson, but others scholars point to a political atmosphere that would certainly raise this possibility:

> For an incumbent president seeking reelection, accomplishments in office provide much of the criteria for evaluation. People make a retrospective judgment, deciding whether or not to vote for a candidate seeking reelection on the basis of how well they believe that candidate and party have performed during the candidate's term of office (Edwards and Wayne 2003).

If it is true that people vote retrospectively (Fiorina 1981), and that they pay attention to issues (e.g., see Key 1966), it is reasonable to assume that this is not lost on presidents. If so, another hypothesis that can be explored is:

H3. In election years, presidents ought to invest an increasing percentage of their non-personal time in social/ceremonial and legislative behaviors.

Using the dataset allows separation and manipulation of the various types of activities needed to explore this hypothesis. The results are in Table 7-5 below. The last column shows that the presidents in this dataset devote just over one third of their non-personal time (time not spent alone or just with family) engaged in social/ceremonial and legislative activities. During their second and fourth years in office — congressional and presidential election years — the percentage jumps to 39.2% and 37.1%, respectively.

Table 7-5: Minutes Spent In Social/Ceremonial And Legislative Activity As A Percentage Of All Non-Personal Activities

Year	Social/ Ceremonial activities	Legislative activities	Social/ Ceremonial + Legislative activities	Other Non-Personal activities[b]	Total non-Personal activities	Percent[c]
1	82968	701	83669	165736	249405	33.5
2	92909	1523	94432	146178	240610	39.2
4	88962	1950	90912	154030	244942	37.1

[a]Executive (includes non-Legislative contacts with Congress and Liaison) and Foreign Policy activities.

[b]Percentage Social/Ceremonial + Legislative activities of Total non-Personal activities.

There appears to be *some* support for this hypothesis, although the increase is slightly higher in *congressional* election years (year 2) than in *presidential* election years (year 4). One caveat: Social/Ceremonial activities (column two) include not only public appearances, but also things like dinner with friends. Legislative activities (column three) *clearly* increase in election years.

Legislative Experience and Activity

One of the advantages of the dataset is that it allows exploration of conflicting suggestions or assumptions about presidential behavior. Rather than letting these conflicts bounce around with no more than an accumulation of anecdotal evidence on any side, activity data provides the ability to at least attempt to systematically resolve such conflicts.

One such conflict would be the effect of a president's background on current behavior. For example, Paul Light (1983) notes that "Eisenhower . . . preferred a hidden-hand approach [to domestic policy making]", and ". . . both Nixon and Carter preferred a detached strategy." On the other hand,

> Lyndon Johnson, Harry Truman, John Kennedy, and Gerald Ford . . . were all involved to one degree or another in the domestic policy process (Light 1983).

What Light does not point out is that these two groups (Nixon and Carter on one hand, and Johnson, Truman, Kennedy, and Ford on the other) break down not only along their level of involvement in domestic policy making, but also along their congressional tenure in the years immediately prior to their entering office. In discussing "personal accessibility to congressional leaders of both parties", James W. Davis and Louis W. Koenig present a remarkably similar list of presidents:

> Despite the major constraints on their time, Presidents Kennedy, Johnson, Ford, and Reagan all maintained an "open presidency," even with members of the opposition party (Davis 1987).

> Lyndon Johnson and Gerald Ford mingled with the legislators most easily; Richard Nixon was the most remote and [Jimmy] Carter [was] somewhat less so (Koenig 1996).

Jimmy Carter never served in Congress, and while Richard Nixon served in both the House and Senate, he was out of Congress for sixteen years (and out of the Vice Presidency for eight years) prior to his becoming president. On the other side, Johnson, Truman, Kennedy, and Ford all were out of Congress for less than four years before becoming president. Kennedy had moved *directly* from the Senate into the White House, while the other three *all* served as Vice President for the entire time between their stints as members of Congress and as President (and that 'entire time' amounted to less than three years for Johnson, and less than a year each for Truman and Ford). The only exception to the rule is Reagan, who, like Carter, had no prior congressional experience.

Distinctions between remarkably similar groups of presidents crop up often in the literature, though there is no evidence of this being the direct focus of examination. Stephen Wayne's (1978) book, *The Legislative Presidency, suggests* that this distinction may play an important part in presidential activity. Wayne notes that the exact same lineup of individuals as Light — presidents Truman, Kennedy, Johnson, and Ford — were much more apt to deal personally with Congress, and much more apt to deal with individual congressmen on a personal level than were presidents Eisenhower and Nixon — and Carter may now be added to their ranks. The former four were all members of Congress at the time of or only a couple of years prior to joining the Executive branch. Of the latter three, Eisenhower had never held public office, and Nixon had not been in Congress for 16 years (he had not been in national government at all for eight), and Carter — being the former governor of Georgia — had neither been in Congress, nor the federal government.

In a more recent work, George Edwards along with Stephen Wayne speak of the relationship between the President and Congress by exemplifying the same two camps:

> On one extreme, Nixon's meetings were often pro forma, serving more as a symbolic ritual than a mechanism for leadership. On the other, Johnson used them as strategy sessions, integrating congressional leaders into the White House legislative liaison operation (Edwards and Wayne 2003).

More recently, a very similar description of Johnson is provided by Robert Dallek:

> One aide recalls: "The best liaison we had with the Congress was Lyndon Johnson. He spent an enormous amount of time persuading congressmen to vote for particular issues." Columnist Drew Pearson, in a memo he wrote to himself, marveled at all the personal attention Johnson was giving to congressmen. "He phones them, writes them notes, draws them aside at receptions to ask their opinions, seeks them out to thank them

for political favors. Almost every Tuesday and Thursday he invites a group of congressmen over for an evening at the White House (Dallek 1998).

Thus it may be that first hand familiarity and identification with a contemporary Congress may in some way affect a president's behavior toward that Congress. In short, these presidents seem to have more contact with Congress. In this case, a reasonably testable hypothesis is:

$H4$. The amount of legislative activity should vary directly with the president's legislative experience.

However, there may be alternative thinking in this area. Given the demands placed on a president's day, they may try to act as efficiently as possible. That is, they may try to spend *less time* in the areas they know well, and concentrate on areas with which they are less familiar. Recall part of the quote from Dwight Eisenhower that opened the first section of this chapter:

> For my part, I early embarked on a program of discussing issues, in a social atmosphere, with groups of congressmen and senators of both parties, in the hope that personal acquaintance would help smooth out difficulties inherent in partisanship (Eisenhower 1963).

Eisenhower *did* ultimately fulfill this plan. Early in his first year, he often (approximately once a week) met with large groups of members of Congress. This type of behavior contradicts the above hypothesis. It is an example of someone with no legislative experience seeking to *increase* his level of legislative interaction. This would lead us to an alternative hypothesis:

$H4_{alt}$. The amount of legislative activity should vary *inversely* with the president's legislative experience.

The definition of Legislative Activity used in coding the database of presidential activities is a rather strict one. Briefly defined, it consists of only those activities designed to influence the outcome of congressional votes. In the absence of any firm indications of this, an activity was coded as Executive and not Legislative activity. Thus, for instance, if a meeting or phone call with a member of Congress was not detailed, it would be coded as an Executive activity. It may be instructive to add another, more loosely-defined variable, called Legislative Contacts, to include *any* contact with a member of Congress not otherwise codeable as Personal, Social/Ceremonial or Foreign Policy activity.

The variable of Legislative Experience loosely answers this question: Did the president accede to his office directly from Congress or the Vice Presidency, or did he come from some place outside government, such as a governorship or the military? Legislative Experience is measured as an index based on whether or not a president has served in Congress, the president's tenure there, any service as vice president, and the time elapsed between serving in the Congress and assuming the presidency.

The first column in Table 7-6 shows the level of legislative experience for each president in the sample. The next four columns present information on data coded as Legislative Activities, and the last two columns present information on data coded as the broader Legislative Contacts category. The number of legislative activities, the amount of time spent in legislative activities, and the amount of time in the more broadly defined legislative "contacts" *all* appear to steadily increase with congressional experience.

Additionally, these numbers appear to remain constant over time. Restricting the data to the first years in office finds that Eisenhower averaged 2.4 activities/month (somewhat lower than, but still similar to, his above overall average of 3.9), Nixon's average was 9.9 (somewhat higher than, but still similar to, his above overall average of 6.9), and Johnson's average was 13.8 (virtually identical to his above overall average of 14.4). Johnson's year as president before his election in 1964 may have led his average to steady out, whereas the others' varied a bit more as they were seeking some sort of a comfortable level of activity. But the important point is that the *direct* relationship between Legislative Experience and Legislative Contacts and Activities obtains throughout a president's time in office.

Table 7-6: Legislative Experience, Activities, and Contacts

Experience Index[a]	Activities	Activities /month	Total time[b]	Time/ month	Contacts[c]	Contacts /month
00.00 (DDE)	45	3.9	365	30.3	291	24.3
06.00 (RMN)	82	6.9	722	60.3	667	55.5
23.50 (LBJ)	171	14.4	3087	257.4	1220	101.7

[a]Years in Congress plus ½ total as Vice President minus years out of government (minimum score of 0).
[b]Total time spent in 'Legislative Activities', measured in minutes.
[c]Legislative contacts are *all* contacts with members of Congress or the Liaison staff (whether or not *type* is coded as *legislative*).

When the data is examined using each month as the unit of analysis, the correlation between Experience and Activities (total minutes per day) is .21 (p<.0001), and between Experience and Contacts (total minutes per month) it is .34 (p<.0001). In other words, there is strong evidence to support H4 over H4$_{alt}$.

There appears to be a direct connection between Congressional experience and Legislative contacts and activity. While not any sort of direct predictive measure of success in office, legislative experience appears to be a decent predictor of the level of interaction between presidents and their congresses.

Other Possibilities

The types of information that may be culled from activity data have been presented so far. The data allow addressing questions about presidential behavior in ways previously closed to research. They allow presidential research to move away from treating each administration as historically unique and further pursue the notion that there are commonalities running through the presidency no matter who happens to be the current occupant. However, there are limits to what can be done with the samples used in compiling the dataset used in this project. A more complete database of presidential activity, encompassing the entire administrations of a wider selection of presidencies will allow addressing even more questions about the presidency. What follows are some brief notations on the limitations of the current dataset, and some possibilities for research with a more complete dataset.

Party

A more complete dataset will help explore questions about the importance of party in Presidential behavior. For example:

H_{party}. Inducement should be more common under party government than under divided government, and Persuasion should be more common under divided government than under party government.

When the two branches are of the same party (party government), there is evidence that the president's behavior when interacting with Congress differs from when they are controlled by different parties (divided government). Specifically, the president's behavior takes on a much more partisan tone. Part of this difference probably stems from the fact that the rewards and punishments dispensed by the president may be more salient to congressmen from his party than to those of the other party. Thus, it can be easily theorized that presidential activity during periods of party government differs from behavior during divided government.

Related to this is the president's electoral performance (especially his "coattails"). Coattail victories, whether they bring in new members or preserve the seats of incumbents, can have significant payoffs for the president in terms of support for the administration's programs (Edwards and Wayne 2003). When presidents can (at least) claim responsibility for their party's electoral success, they may very well act differently than when they are seen as a liability.

When examining the data to see if there is any support for this hypothesis, the simplest thing to say is that the data are ambiguous. Yet, given the limited sample, this hypothesis cannot yet be ruled out. Table 7-7 shows the average amount of time devoted to persuasion and inducement per 120-day sample.

Table 7-7: Average Time (in Minutes) Spent in Persuasion and Inducement Activities Under Party and Divided Government

PTYGOV[a]	Persuasion	Inducement	Pitch (Persuasion + Inducement)
0(Divided Gov.)	44.75	28	72.75
1(Party Gov.)	378.4	23	401.4

[a]PTYGOV is a dummy variable: 0 if the president and Congress are of different parties, and 1 if they are of the same party.

The data consist of average sums in minutes for each sample. There are 9 overall samples — 3 each for 3 presidents. Four of these samples are classified as divided government (DDE 56; RMN 69, 70, 72) and five are classified as party government (DDE 53, 54; LBJ 65, 66, 68). The one, glaringly apparent fact is that, on average, these presidents were *much* more active in terms of pitching during times of party government, and that the vast majority of those pitches were persuasive in nature. Certainly one cannot say from the evidence so far that inducement is more common than persuasion under party government and vice versa. However, of these three presidents, only Eisenhower served during periods of *both* party *and* divided government. It may be helpful to examine his "pitching record". When the data are limited to his samples (1953, 1954, and 1956) a different picture emerges as shown in Table 7-8.

Table 7-8: Average Time (in Minutes) Spent In Persuasion And Inducement Activities Under Party And Divided Government — Eisenhower Administration Only

PTYGOV	Persuasion	Inducement	Pitch (Persuasion + Inducement)
0 (Divided Gov.)	66	10	76
1 (Party Gov.)	51	30.5	81.5

The data for party government are averaged across two samples (1953 and 1954). The data for divided government are totals from the 1956 sample. It appears that Eisenhower's pitching activity was fairly constant across both divided and party government. In addition, while persuasion was the more common tactic in both situations, inducement was more than three times more likely to occur under party government than it was under divided government, while persuasion was slightly more likely to occur under divided government than it was under party government. This portion of the data clearly supports H3. One caution though: the Pearson correlations between PTYGOV and Persuasion (-.14) and Inducement (.10) are in the expected directions, but they are not significant.

The overall data may be skewed by the Johnson data. He is acknowledged as having been an unusually active president. This holds true in the legislative activity data of this study as well. Of the 2298 minutes devoted by all three presidents to pitching activities, 1790, or 78%, were Johnson's. Since 98% of all *his* pitches involved persuasion, this adds a tremendous skew to the data. As data are gathered on a wider variety of presidents (especially ones who serve under both party and divided governments, like Truman and Clinton), perhaps a truer picture will emerge. Right now, the best that may be said is that, while the Eisenhower data appears to support H3, the data currently available are really not comprehensive enough for a definitive answer. Future analysis of data from the Truman and Clinton (when it becomes available) administrations will certainly help to clarify the effects of party control over each branch.

Chapter 8: Results II

Contact Data

A subset of the activity data is useful in order to more fully focus on contact with Congress. This subset consists of the activities where the variable LEGCONT (presidential contact with a member of Congress; see p.95) >0. In this dataset, the unit of analysis shifts from the president's activities to the individual House and Senate member of these Congresses. Each member's LEGCONT is totaled for the sample periods in each Congress. In other words, there is now have a second dataset of presidential contact with each member of Congress over the sample time periods.

Contact Data and the Case of Wilbur Mills

What is available through this second dataset? Information specifically on whom the president is contacting, when, and for how long. This exposes who in Congress has the president's ear and who doesn't. This allows exploring any patterns in congressional contact. Are there any similarities among those contacted? Among those ignored?

In addition, it is also possible to track the interaction between individual members of Congress and presidents over several administrations. This may be demonstrated by examining the contact over time between one member of Congress and the sample presidents. This example may best be called 'the rise and fall of Wilbur Mills'.

Figure 8-1 displays the amount of contact Rep. Wilbur Mills (D-Ark.) had with each of the presidents during the sample periods. The contact data provides a graphic representation of Rep. Mills' access to the three presidents in the sample. There is only one contact during the Eisenhower sample, frequent contact during the Johnson sample, and only sporadic contact during the Nixon sample. The lone instance in the Eisenhower sample is a mass introductory gathering with members of Congress conducted early in the administration. The dramatic increase in frequency during the Johnson sample probably reflects three things: Johnson's tremendous activity, the Democratic Party's majority status, and Rep. Mills' growing influence as the now Chair of the Ways and Means Committee. Finally, the up-and-down nature of the contact with Nixon most likely reflects Nixon's reluctant contact with an influential member of the opposite, but majority, party.

Figure 8-1: Legislative Contact of Wilbur Mills Over Three Administrations

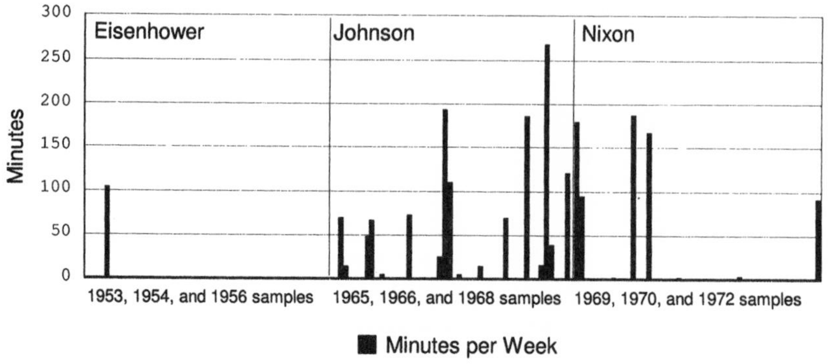

■ Minutes per Week

This illustrates the type of information may be culled from the Contact data. Now it is time to put the data to substantive use.

Contact Data Analysis

To simplify the analysis done in this section, only the first Congress of each administration is used (that would be the 83rd, 89th, and 91st Congresses). This leaves a dataset of approximately 1650 cases (members serving in more than one of the above congresses are treated as separate entries for each Congress).

There is now information as to who the President had contact with, and for how long. The next step is to put the contact data to use. There are two ways in which to use contact data. First, as a dependent variable, the data may be used to explore the factors leading presidents to contact some members of Congress more than others. Second, as an independent variable, the data may be used to explore the usefulness of contacts in the legislative arena. This section is devoted to exploring these two possibilities. One note:

while the data in this study are sufficient to explore the former (contact as a dependent variable), there is not yet enough data to *thoroughly* pursue the latter (contact as an independent variable). Nonetheless, some useful inquiries can and will be made into using contact data as an independent variable.

Dependent Variable

The question to be explored is basically, 'what produces variations in presidential contact?' More informally, the question is essentially, 'what causes presidents to contact some members of Congress more than others?' Earlier in this study, the question of overall levels of contact was addressed. It was found that presidents' legislative experience affects their level of overall contact. From this it may be surmised that contact with individual members of Congress is also connected to the legislative process.

To begin addressing this question of variations in contact, it is useful to look at what presidents themselves have to say.

In his presidential memoirs, Dwight Eisenhower appears to connect influence in Congress with congressional leadership. He claimed that

> of all the mechanisms for developing coordination between the White House and the Congress — particularly with the Republican members — by far the most effective was the weekly meeting I held with the *Legislative leaders* (emphasis added). (Eisenhower 1963)

Lyndon Johnson sees a similar linkage. In his presidential memoirs, Johnson says that when he assumed office in 1963, what he wanted to do was

> to try to unify the leaders in the administration, the leaders in the two parties, and the *leaders in the Congress* — for a while at least, until we could get Congress into action (emphasis added). (Johnson 1971)

It is clear from these passages, that they saw a connection between contact with congressional leaders and influencing Congress. From this, it may be assumed that leadership positions within Congress play a part in explaining contact variation. In other words,

H_{leader}: **Presidential contact with members of Congress is greater among congressional leaders than among other members of Congress.**

This hypothesis may be examined by comparing the average amount of time spent in contact with congressional leaders to that of rank and file members. Leadership here is defined as those members holding the positions of

Speaker of the House, House and Senate Floor Leaders, and House and Senate Assistant Floor Leaders ("Whips"). The results below clearly show that Eisenhower and Johnson lived up to their words. Fewer than two percent of Congress received more than 20 percent of all presidential contacts over the sample periods. Presidents were in contact with congressional leaders an average that is more than 15 times greater than that spent with rank and file members. One might say that leadership has its privileges.

Table 8-1: Presidential Contact With Congressional Leaders And Rank And File

	Number	S Contact[a]	% Contact	Average Contact[a]
Leadership	28	37304.0	22.4	1332.3
Rank & File	1,619	129462.5	77.6	80.0

[a] Per member, in minutes

The correlation between leadership position and contact is a strong one. The Pearson correlation coefficients for each administration are both statistically significant and strong. For Eisenhower it is .58; for Johnson it is .67; and for Nixon it is .50[14]. Examining the contact with only leaders of the president's party reveals even stronger correlations: .81 for Eisenhower; .81 for Johnson; and .57 for Nixon[15].

Basic Regression Model

Finally, the prominence of leadership positions become all the more apparent when a regression model is tested using several independent variables. For this model, several independent variables are introduced:

- **Congress** (This is quite simply the number of the Congresses included in the sample — the 83rd, 89th, and 91st. It is included to test for the presence of any long-term trends)
- **Political Party**
- **President's Party** (a dummy variable where members of the president's party are coded as 1 and all others as 0)
- **Leadership** (as explained earlier)
- **President's Leader** (a dummy consisting of only those leaders, as defined above, of the president's party)
- **Committee Chair**

---

[14] p<.001 for each. Nixon's lower number is likely due to serving under an opposition Congress.
[15] p<.001 for each.

- **Ranking Minority Committee Member**
- **President's Committee Leader** (another dummy where the top ranking committee member of the president's party for each standing committee is coded as 1 and all others as 0)
- **ADA** ratings
- **President's ADA** ratings (coded as ADA ratings for Democratic presidents and (100 - ADA) for Republican presidents)
- and finally Keith Poole's **NOMINATE** dimensions (Poole 1991)

These independent variables produce a model with an *r* of .68, an *r-squared* of .47, and an *adjusted r-squared* of .46. Table 8-2 shows the results of this model. Apparently, by far the strongest factors are what might be called 'leadership' variables. The most statistically significant variables (p<.001) are the Leadership, President's Leadership, and President's Committee Leader variables (along with Ranking Member (p=.001) and President's ADA (p=.002).

Table 8-2: Regression Coefficients Of Presidential Contact Model

	Unstandardized Coefficients		Standardized Coefficients	t	Sig.
	B	Std. Error	Beta		
(Constant)	-378.298	495.319		-0.764	0.445
CONG	3.805	5.548	0.018	0.686	0.493
PARTY	0.262	0.174	0.060	1.501	0.134
PP	21.088	12.890	0.049	1.636	0.102
LDR	338.797	56.156	0.181	6.033	0.000*
PRES.LDR	1327.811	85.250	0.465	15.576	0.000*
CC	32.996	24.343	0.048	1.355	0.176
RM	27.070	26.304	0.098	3.310	0.001
PRES.CL	160.541	28.743	0.182	5.585	0.000*
ADA	-0.103	0.368	-0.017	-0.279	0.781
PRES.ADA	0.511	0.167	0.085	3.057	0.002
NOM1	-20.160	46.970	-0.030	-0.429	0.668
NOM2	26.965	24.354	0.029	1.107	0.268

* p<.001

Several of these variables are neither statistically significant in this model, nor is at least one significantly correlated with presidential contact. As such, it might be useful to alter the model somewhat to see if the overall fit improves. The first candidate for change is the deletion of NOM2 (Poole's 2nd dimension — roughly equivalent to ideology within party). This variable is neither significant in the regression model, nor is it significantly correlated with contact. When this is done, the fit remains identical ($r = .68$, r-$squared = .47$, adjusted r-$squared = .46$).

The next candidate for exclusion is the Ranking Member variable. While this variable is significantly correlated with contact, the coefficient is a scant .095. However, when this variable is excluded, the overall fit of the model actually drops slightly (though negligibly).

If we turn around and begin excluding variables based on the regression results in Table 8-2, the fit varies little. For example, dropping the three least related variables, ADA, NOM1, and CONG, produces a fit virtually identical to the overall model.

Optimal Regression Model

There is only one situation in which fit of the model is noticeably improved. This is when the ADA and President's ADA variables are removed. While appearing counterintuitive at first blush, this alteration is defensible. The ADA variable is more logically explored when controlling for administration. Lumping presidents of differing ideological perspectives would produce a canceling effect explaining the lack of significance in the original model.

Dropping the President's ADA variable is a bit more problematic to explain. In this variable, the scores are corrected so everyone is facing in the same ideological direction so to speak. This would account for the President's ADA variable being a much stronger one than simple ADA in the regression model. What is best said about ADA overall is that it is only weakly correlated with contact in any event. While statistically significant, and in the expected directions, the correlations are *very weak* at best. For Johnson, the correlation coefficient is .11, and for Nixon, it is -.16. From these numbers, and from the presidential quotes noted earlier, it appears that being an ideological soul mate of the president's does not do a member of Congress much good unless that person has the leadership position with which to 'deliver the goods' for the president. Thus, the ADA variables are dropped from the model.

When this is done, this 'optimal' model produces a noticeably improved *r* of .76, an *r-squared* of .58, and an *adjusted r-squared* of .58 as well.

Through all of this model-tinkering, the significant variables remain virtually unchanged. Under the 'optimal' model, as well as under the original model, there are a handful of variables that explain the lion's share of variation in presidential contact. While the overall fit of the 'optimal' model does improve, this regression model produces similar results in terms of significant independent variables. Table 8-3 shows some shifting of weights, but the same three 'leadership' variables, Leadership, President's Leadership, and President's Congressional Leadership stand out as the strongest variables in the model.

There is clear support for the hypothesis regarding presidential contact. The statements by Eisenhower and Johnson noted earlier can be empirically verified using contact data.

One interesting note: in the optimized model, Congress has become a significant variable (albeit the weakest of any significant variable). In other words, there appears to be some long-term trend in contact with Congress. Since the Beta is negative, the results mean that presidential contact with Congress has dropped over time. This presents an intriguing area for further exploration, but given the scope of the current dataset, there may be less than meets the eye.

Eisenhower was quoted earlier in this project as saying he set about early on in his administration to meet with as many members of Congress as possible. Since the data used here include only samples from the first two years of each administration, Eisenhower's contact with Congress may indeed be overstated. This, combined with Johnson's natural energy, and Nixon's aloofness (also discussed earlier), may very well account for the apparent inverse relationship between time and contact. At any rate, this remains an intriguing area for future research.

Presidential Contact as a Dependent Variable

The regression model shows that the variables that far outpace all others are combination partisan/leadership variables (i.e. being the highest ranking committee member of the president's party or being the highest ranking party leaders of the president's party). Presidents appear to devote *far* more of contact to congressional leaders — and especially leaders of their own party — than to anyone else in Congress. In terms of presidential activity in the legislative arena, the old saying, "it's not what you know, it's who you know" appears to be quite correct. In order to better fit current concerns, maybe it could be altered to read "it's not what you believe, it's who you are"!

Presidential Legislative Activity

Table 8-3: Regression Coefficients Of Optimized Presidential Contact Model

	Unstandardized Coefficients		Standardized Coefficients	t	Sig.
	B	Std. Error	Beta		
(Constant)	1023.483	118.358		8.647	0.000***
CONG	-11.820	1.333	-0.143	-8.869	0.000***
PARTY	0.438	0.158	0.078	2.776	0.006**
PP	25.513	10.281	0.045	2.482	0.013*
LDR	254.599	50.014	0.112	5.091	0.000***
PRES.LDR	1938.042	69.967	0.611	27.699	0.000***
CC	64.841	25.683	0.056	2.525	0.012*
RM	42.236	22.056	0.036	1.915	0.056
PRES.CL	168.858	27.838	0.146	6.066	0.000***
NOM1	-2.957	22.194	-0.003	-0.133	0.894
NOM2	59.631	21.330	0.052	2.796	0.005**

*** $p<.001$
** $p<.01$
* $p<.05$

Legislative Activity and Contact as Independent Variables

So far, the legislative contact and activity data have been examined as a dependent variable. However, part of the purpose of developing the dataset is to help refine the notion of presidential influence in the legislative arena. As such, the data must help explain the success or failure of presidential interaction with Congress.

A hypothesis to test is laid out for exploration by Lyn Ragsdale (1998). In explaining why presidents need political scientists, she says, "Political scientists offer presidents generalizations about White House relations with . . . Congress." In doing so, she provides this hypothesis:

> The higher the president's level of legislative activity (that is, the more pieces of legislation on which he takes a position) the lower his legislative success. Conversely, the lower the activity, the more successful is the president.

She derives this hypothesis from the work of Charles Ostrom and Dennis Simon (1985). In their studies, they note that "[i]ncreases in [the president's legislative] activity will produce a decline in success [on Congressional votes] at the rate of 1.8 points for every 100 presidential position votes". This finding was derived from a multivariate model designed to both predict levels of public approval and to explore its associated effect on legislative success.

One of the main reasons for developing the dataset used in this project is to move beyond simple presidential position-taking toward a fuller exploration of the president's actions. The exploration should yield information on whether or not the president is actually *doing* anything to back up the positions taken, and whether or not doing something has any effect. This would seem to be an opportune moment to apply this notion. As such, the next hypothesis to explore in this project is the Ostrom and Simon hypothesis as reiterated by Lyn Ragsdale.

H_{active}: **The president's success rate in Congress varies inversely with the president's level of legislative activity.**

Unlike the Ostrom and Simon hypothesis, however, the definition of legislative activity will be the more literal one (activity) used throughout this project as opposed to Ostrom and Simon's definition (position-taking).

It should be said up front that there is really insufficient data available in the activity dataset to *fully* explore this hypothesis. However, a quick inquiry may prove informative. To do so, it is necessary to return to the original activity dataset and to look at the amount of legislative activities for each sample period in the dataset, comparing them to measures of presidential success in Congress. Both the Legislative Activity and the broader Legislative Contact data will be used. A comparison of absolute counts of legislative activity to success rates, as seen in Table 8-4, yields little in the way of an answer to the hypothesis. The correlation between Legislative Activity and *CQ* vote success scores is a mere 0.2 and there is no correlation between Activity and *CQ* legislative success scores. The correlations for Legislative Contacts are somewhat stronger — 0.4 for vote success and 0.1 for legislative success — but they are still very weak. One problem with using the data in this way is that it does not account for overall levels of presidential activity (see below). As has been noted, Lyndon Johnson and Richard Nixon were *much* more active than was Dwight Eisenhower. Simply looking at absolute levels fails to account for this and may yield a misleading picture — Johnson's amounts of legislative activity are certain to be far greater than either Eisenhower or Nixon no matter what level of legislative success he achieved.

A better picture is painted when considering the *percentage of the president's workday devoted to legislative activity* (regardless of how big that workday is). If we examine the *percentage* of legislative behavior in the president's workday a different picture emerges (see Table 8-5, below).

Table 8-4: Comparison Of Presidential Legislative Activity And Legislative Success Rates

President	Year	Legis. Acts[a]	Legis. Cont[a]	Success on Votes[b]	Success on Legislation[c]
Eisenhower	1	10	128	89.0%	72.7%
Eisenhower	2	23	117	82.8	64.7
Eisenhower	4	12	46	70	45.7
Johnson	1	48	456	93	68.9
Johnson	2	60	388	79	55.8
Johnson	4	63	377	75	55.8
Nixon	1	46	292	74	32.2
Nixon	2	26	309	77	46.1
Nixon	4	10	66	66	44

[a]Number of activities recorded during the sample period.
[b]*Congressional Quarterly.*
[c]*Congressional Quarterly.* This statistic was discontinued after 1975 because of validity problems.

Table 8-5 provides this picture. Correlations for the *percentage* of legislative behavior are much more noticeable. The correlation between the percentage of Legislative Activities and vote success is a modest 0.4, as it is with legislative success as well. The correlations for Legislative Contacts are much stronger however. The correlation between the percentage of Legislative Contacts and vote success is 0.8, and the correlation between the percentage of Contacts and legislative success is 0.7. These correlations indicate that presidents enjoy greater success in Congress when they have more contact with Congress — the opposite of what Ostrom and Simon found.

There are a couple of caveats, however. First, the above exploration is based on very limited data. With an *N* of 9, virtually no correlation is going to be statistically significant. Second, the "model" looks only at legislative activity and success in Congress. This is certainly a seriously underspecified model. Presidential approval ratings, party control of the two branches, and many other factors ought to be included in any model of presidential success.

These having been noted however, this early study *does* indicate the value of contact with Congress to a president interested in pursuing a legislative agenda.

Table 8-5: Comparison Of Presidential Legislative Activity (As A Percentage Of The Presidential Workday) And Legislative Success Rates

President	Year	% Legis. Acts[a]	% Legis. Cont[a]	Success on Votes[b]	Success on Legis.[c]
Eisenhower	1	1.0%	12.5%	89.0%	72.7%
Eisenhower	2	2	10.4	82.8	64.7
Eisenhower	4	0.6	2.5	70	45.7
Johnson	1	0.8	7.9	93	68.9
Johnson	2	1	6.3	79	55.8
Johnson	4	1.1	6.7	75	55.8
Nixon	1	1	6.5	74	32.2
Nixon	2	0.5	6.5	77	46.1
Nixon	4	0.3	1.7	66	44

[a]Legislative behavior as a percentage of workday.
[b]*Congressional Quarterly.*
[c]*Congressional Quarterly.* This statistic was discontinued after 1975 because of validity concerns.

The Value of Contact? Lyndon Johnson and Medicare

It is already well established, both here and elsewhere, that, as president, Lyndon Johnson was deeply involved in the legislative process. Doris Kearns (1974) says that "[o]ther presidents had paid close attention to the Congress, but the scope and intensity of Lyndon Johnson's participation in the legislative process were unprecedented." Of Johnson, she also says,

he had to know how much to involve which members of Congress in what bill, selecting for each member the kind of participation that promised him the greatest reward, deciding where to draw the line in order to avoid the kind of overinvolvement that might expose his program to crippling opposition in advance. And he had to know these things himself, directly, from face-to-face talks, because only Johnson was in contact with all the varied groups and subgroups in both Congress and the administration (Kearns 1974).

She quotes Johnson as saying that

> There is but one way for a President to deal with the Congress, and that is continuously, incessantly, and without interruption. If it's really going to work, the relationship between the President and the Congress has got be almost incestuous. He's got to know them even better than they know themselves. And then, on the basis of this knowledge, he's got to build a system that stretches from the cradle to the grave, from the moment a bill is introduced to the moment it is officially enrolled as the law of the land (Kearns 1974).

It is clear that Johnson believed that contact with Congress was the key to influence in the legislative arena. In the previous section, we saw that there may be some merit to his thinking. There is at least some correlation between contact and legislative success on the aggregate level.

The next step is to see if the same notion holds true in individual instances. In other words, can the value of contact be demonstrated in any particular instance? Is there any evidence that presidential contact with members of Congress played any part in getting a piece of legislation passed? The exploration of these questions is necessarily tentative, given the nature of the current dataset. However, the steps taken here to explore these questions are valuable in that they move toward empirical verification of Johnson's and Kearn's statements. To do this requires again using the contact data developed in the last chapter.

The first step is to select a bill. The first factor to consider in selecting a bill is timing. A bill that went through floor debate during the periods of time covered in the contact data must be located. This will provide at least some reasonable expectation of some relationship between the bill and the recorded contact.

Second, since the contact data does not detail the content of contact, only the amount, it is impossible to determine whether any contact is related to a particular piece of legislation. Given this limitation, it is best to select a prominent bill, one that dominated the political landscape during its existence. This will provide some confidence that a large amount of the contacts recorded are connected to the legislation being considered.

A contemporary example of a proposal fitting the above criteria would be President Clinton's 1993 economic package. Had the contact samples — which remember, run from January 20th through May 19th of the sampled years — included 1993, the Clinton package would qualify on the first count because it was voted on in May of 1993. It would qualify on the second count because it was virtually the sole focus of both ends of Pennsylvania Avenue during its time before the floors of the House and Senate.

Fortunately there are bills from which to choose. One bill that meets both criteria was the Medicare Act of 1965. It passed the House on April 8th, 1965 and the Senate later that summer. The House activity falls within the 89th Congress contact sample. In addition, it was a high priority item. Lyndon Johnson repeatedly emphasized the importance of Medicare:

> Throughout the 1964 Presidential campaign I repeatedly promised that medical care for the elderly would be "at the top of my list" of proposals to the new Congress. . . .

> In my State of the Union message on January 4 [1965], I asked the Eighty-ninth Congress to make Medicare its first order of business. . . .

> To dramatize the importance we attached to it, we asked the leadership to designate it "S-1" in the Senate . . . and "HR-1" in the House (Johnson 1971).

It is clear from Johnson's own words that he felt Medicare was of primary importance. At the time, *Congressional Quarterly* noted this as well, referring to the Medicare bill as "the President's top priority legislative request for 1965" ("Ways and Means. . . " 1965). Robert Dallek also notes that, "[f]or Johnson, there could be no Great Society — no improved quality of national life — without greater access for all Americans to health care . . . . A prime Johnson concern was to assure that a Medicare law would pass the 89th Congress." (Dallek 1998).

It appears that the Medicare bill is an appropriate one to use. The question to be addressed is whether or not there is a relationship between the amount presidential contact with a member of Congress and their vote on the Medicare bill. To address this, the contact dataset will be adjusted to fit the requirements of the question.

The contact dataset must be adjusted in five ways:

- First, it needs to be restricted to the 89th Congress (for obvious reasons).
- Second, the study will be limited House activity, since floor debate on Medicare took place at different times in the House and in the Senate (and, as noted above, the Senate vote did not take place until the summer of 1965, well after the 89th Congress contact data sample).

- Third, it needs to be restricted to a small window of time *within* the 89th Congress sample. All contact data after the House vote on Medicare is irrelevant. In addition, the further back in time we go before the House vote, the less relevant the data. So, the data will be restricted to approximately the month before the House vote.

- Fourth, the data will be limited to only those members of Congress with whom Johnson had had any contact with during the sample period. The reason for this is that, quite simply, even with all the talk about the importance of interaction, Johnson only had *direct* contact with a relatively few members of the House (amounting to approximately 10% of the House), leaving the rest to interact with the liaison staff. Given a modal level of contact of 0 among the entire House, no analysis would return any meaningful results. And given the focus on what is essentially the *value* of contact, a focus on only those with whom he *did* contact can help tell us whether or not contact with others would boost his support if needed.

- Finally, the Congressional Leadership (as defined earlier) will be eliminated from the sample. It is, again, impossible from this dataset to disaggregate contact related to Medicare from unrelated contact. While choosing a prominent issue like Medicare does boost the likelihood that any given contact will concern that topic, the leadership are much more likely than the rank and file to be contacted on any number of matters at any given time period. It is more probable that the rank and file will be contacted solely concerning legislation of the moment.

Limiting the dataset to those House rank and file with whom the president had had some contact during the sample leaves us with 49 members. Among those members, there is a mild but statistically significant relationship between the amount of contact a House member received from the president in the month before the Medicare vote and that member's vote on the Medicare bill. The correlation coefficient is .29 ($p<.05$). While it again must be noted that there is 'noise' in this data (it is virtually certain that Medicare, wile prominent, was not the *sole* topic of contact), there does appear to be some relationship between contact and vote. Perhaps if the data could be 'filtered' to focus only on the bill at hand (in this case, Medicare) a more definitive answer would be forthcoming. What *is* apparent is that the ability to predict the Medicare vote of the rank and file House members *is* somewhat enhanced by knowing how much contact they had with Johnson.

While this initial inquiry appears to support Johnson's beliefs, too much should not be read into these results. The saying, 'correlation does not imply causation' clearly applies here. The temporal sequence is good. All contact

Lyndon Johnson signs the 1965 Medicare bill (LBJ Library)

does indeed precede the vote on Medicare. However, we have not eliminated any potential outside causes.

For example, while there is a mild correlation between contact and vote, there are strong and statistically significant correlations between both party and ADA scores and the Medicare vote. The correlation coefficient between party (Democrat = 1, Republican = 0) and Medicare vote among those contacted by Johnson is .42 (p<.01), and the correlation coefficient between ADA score and Medicare vote among those contacted by Johnson is .74 (p<.01). The nature of these numbers suggest that many members of Congress may be 'predisposed' to support Medicare, regardless of contact.

Placing contact, party, and ADA score into a regression model with Medicare vote as the dependent variable explains a good portion of the variance in Medicare vote among those contacted by Johnson (r = .75, r-squared = .56, adjusted r-squared = .53), but only the ADA score stands up as a significant independent variable (see Table 8-6, below). Contact washes out completely as an explanatory variable.

The jury on the value of contact in any *individual* instance is still out. There appears to be a mild relationship between contact and the Medicare vote, but the evidence does not point to any causal relationship on this individual level. A wider variety of legislation ought to be considered before any firm pronouncements are made in this area.

Table 8-6: Regression Analysis Of Medicare Vote.

	Standardized Beta	t	Significance
(Constant)		1.616	0.113
PARTY	-0.060	-0.544	0.589
ADA	0.701	6.222	0.000*
CONTACT	0.060	0.617	0.540

*p<.001

A Consideration for Future Exploration

As noted earlier, legislative activities *clearly* increase in election years. This *may* be because presidents believe that legislative accomplishment (or at least the appearance of involvement) is a salient item among the voting public. However, a closer examination of the dataset reveals a serious caveat: this finding is clearly driven by the Johnson data. He exhibited so many more legislative activities, that whatever pattern emerged in his data, it could sometimes be reflected in the combined data of all three presidents no matter what patterns the other two presidents may have shown. In fact, examining the three presidents in the sample separately finds that Nixon and Eisenhower did not follow this pattern at all (see Table 8-7, below). Eisenhower peaks during the second year, and Nixon's pattern is, to a certain extent, the *opposite* of what was predicted. Only Johnson follows the predicted pattern, and his activity levels are so much greater than the other two that they severely skew the overall data. This appears to highlight the need for data on a much larger scale. Data on third years and additional presidents will help clear up questions like the one raised here.

Table 8-7: Amount Of Legislative Activities By Year And Administration

Year	Eisenhower Legislative activities[a]	Johnson Legislative activities	Nixon Legislative activities
1	50	283	368
2	233	1024	266
3	na	na	na
4	82	1780	88

[a]All activity entries are in minutes.

Summary

It now appears not only possible, but quite easy to move in the more systematic direction suggested by King and Ragsdale earlier.

Presidential activity *can* be systematically gathered, assessed, and used to answer questions about behavior. As such, research may move closer to the notion of exploring true influence in the legislative arena.

It is also clear from the data that presidents are *not* unique individuals, and their behavior *can* be assessed above and beyond a simple personality profile. This is not to say that personality is unimportant (as is suggested below), but rather to say that it is not the *only* factor explaining behavior in the Oval Office.

Chapter 9: Discussion

This book begins with a discussion of what is expected of our presidents. It is clear that they are expected to be legislative leaders. It is also clear that presidents (and presidential candidates) are indeed aware of this expectation. To address this notion of leadership, this project considers the question of what presidents do — in a literal sense — to meet this expectation. The last two chapters provide many results in an inquiry into presidential activity. So, the questions here are: What has been learned?; and What does this say about presidential leadership in the American system?

What Has Been Learned?

Analyses of activity data points in the following directions:

- At the beginning of an administration, presidents devote more of their legislative activity to organization than at subsequent points in time.
- Legislatively inexperienced presidents are likely to devote more of their legislative activity to plotting strategy than to the actual 'sales pitch'.
- There is a direct connection between presidents' legislative experience and the level of their legislative contact.
- Legislative activities clearly increase in election years.
- While it is not clear that the partisan composition of the Congress alone affects the president's legislative activity, nor is it clear that ideology has any effect as well, it *is* clear that such activity is directed squarely at the institutional, partisan and committee *leadership* in Congress.

- Finally, there appears to be at least some evidence of a direct relationship between contact and success.

Presidential Leadership in the American System

These results appear to provide a (rather unusually shaped!) three-paned window through which to view presidential leadership. Much like 'polarized' lenses, the presidency appears differently when looking through each of the panes. The first pane is developmental — a view of the incumbent's journey toward becoming *the* president. The second pane is organizational — a view of how the president fits into the legislative process. The third pane is a commentary on democratic theory in an American setting — do the American people really get what they want?

The Developmental Pane. Activity analysis points to a learning curve in the presidency. By no means is this any sort of earth-shattering news, but there is empirical evidence of behavioral changes over time. The analysis also provides the ability to pinpoint exactly what those changes are.

Analysis of activity data indicate that presidents without much experience in the national legislative arena do not immediately dive into it seeking victory. They appear to hold back, engaging in internal strategy — what one might call a period of initial introspection. Individual differences among legislative tyros do appear as they 'mature', but they diversify from a similar starting point. In the data at hand, the legislative outsiders — Eisenhower and Nixon both began presidential life as outside strategizers whereas the legislative professional — Johnson — entered the middle of the arena from the very start.

In addition, all presidents appear to begin their administrations with a period of organization, in a sense, preparing to do battle.

So, it seems that there is not only a ceremonial inauguration, but a substantive, legislative inauguration as well. More importantly, is appears that the character and length of that period of time will differ among administrations depending on the incumbent's level of prior legislative experience. This is something to consider when heading to the ballot box.

The Organizational Pane. Presidents play an important role in the legislative arena. Not only has this role become institutionalized (especially in the latter part of the 20th century), but the actual structure of the Executive Branch has developed in ways designed to accommodate this institutionalized role. The Office of Congressional Relations (also referred to as the Congressional Liaison) was born informally under the Eisenhower administration and has subsequently grown and formalized to address and reflect this growing institutionalization.

Activity analysis points to the benefits of contact between presidents and their congresses. It also points directly to the prominence of contact between presidents and congressional leadership. Barbara Sinclair (1997) talks of the recent (since the 1970s) growth in "summitry" or "[r]elatively formal negotiations between congressional leaders" and the White House. It appears from the activity data that some form of summitry has been occurring for much longer periods of time. Given the value of contact to a president, not only is the liaison office a worthwhile addition to the president, but some further institutionalization of contact with the leadership may have additional benefits.

An interesting thought occurs upon considering this. There may be benefits not only to the process, but also to the broader environment. Cynicism about national government is rampant, and has been for much of the last three decades. The perception (oftentimes correct!) of institutional competition and of partisan squabbling in an era of divided government are usually the driving forces behind this cynicism. Would more joint activity by the president and the congressional leadership help to reverse this trend? If the public values legislative activity of one form or another, and if Sinclair's "summitry" helps promote this, then it may be useful to institutionalize some sort of *public, joint* appearances between the President and congressional leaders. This might become the American equivalent of Prime Minister's questions (though not as one-sided).

The Commentary. If, as is pointed out at the beginning of this project, Americans look to presidents as legislative leaders; and if they want legislative action, then the results of the activity analysis speak well for democracy in an American context. Quite simply, national elections give the public what it wants. Americans may or may not *realize* this. They may or may not *like* what they get — but they *do* get it.

How is this the case? The answer is that elections foster contact between the White House and Capitol Hill, and there is at least some evidence here that that produces legislative results.

Remember, one of the first propositions in this project is that Americans view their presidents as legislative leaders. Presidents are pressed for legislative solutions and they are judged on their ability to deliver. As noted above, presidents and presidential candidates are well aware of this. In the activity analysis, it is clear that presidents alter their behavior during election years — they engage in greater amounts of legislative activity. Concurrently, the analysis provides evidence that contact with Congress varies directly with a president's success in the legislative arena. The authors of the Constitution provided for elections in order to promote accountability and a sense of popular influence[16]. This project appears to vindicate their thinking. Americans want presidents to be active in the legislative arena, and elections promote such activity.

The Bottom Line

In sum, activity analysis provides both theoretical and applied knowledge. Hypotheses on presidential behavior may be tested: What affects behavior? What does behavior affect? Activity analysis allows for organizational and structural recommendations: Should the Office of Congressional Relations be restructured? What should its mission be? Are new structures needed? Americans may also have a better idea of what to look for in a presidential candidate: What backgrounds are valuable? Business? Military? State government? Congress?

The past two decades have provoked serious evaluations and reevaluations of the institution of the presidency. Controversial wars, scandals, impeachment proceedings, partisan and ideological divisions litter the presidential landscape. These events show no sign of abating at that start of the new century. The ability to analyze the Executive Branch — and to act on that analysis must be kept current. Activity analysis allows research to make new inroads into the presidency. It also allows old ideas to be examined from new perspectives. It opens up to political scientists a wealth of data (in presidential libraries) that was heretofore the province of journalists and historians. It provides the ability to tell the stories that need telling, and to additionally learn from those stories preparing for the future.

---

[16] See *Federalist* #68

Chapter 10: 'Quantitative Biography' and the Future

Creating the presidential activity datasets in effect means writing "quantitative biographies". Aside from the immediate task at hand (developing a measure to help further explore the question of legislative influence), the question underlying this chapter is, "Are Quantitative Biographies useful in any other way?" The quick answer is that the institution of the presidency is more prominent than ever, and that this prominence both fosters and necessitates a concurrent evolution in presidential research. As the 19th century has been called the century of the legislature, so the 20th century is the century of the executive. This is as true in the United States as it is anywhere else. The latter half of the 20th century especially has seen the growth of the presidency, both in physical and psychological size. As an appropriate attendant of this growth, there has been increasing attention paid to the presidency by political scientists. Alongside this shift in attention is a change in focus from descriptive accounts to more rigorously analytical ones (as noted previously in this project).

This new emphasis is proper, but as with any new venture, associated problems become apparent. One of the biggest obstacles facing presidential scholars today is the idiosyncratic nature of much of the literature on the office. Since most observable and *measurable* activities in the White House (such as vetoes, cabinet meetings, and executive and judicial appointments) are either peripheral or offer less than a complete assessment of the office, those searching for more rigorous explanations of the presidency are left wanting for something to grasp. Enter "quantitative biography".

Cliometrics

"Cliometrics" is a term historians use for methodologically rigorous explorations of history. Much of the discipline of political science, including presidential studies, is becoming more cliometric in nature. That is, it is changing over time from largely historical and biographical explorations to more methodologically rigorous ones. This is evident in the proliferation of statistical studies of the presidency — ranging from analysis of vetoes to the growing studies of presidential influence in the legislative arena. The rationale for this movement was set out in a convincing fashion by Gary King and Lyn Ragsdale in the introduction of their book *The Elusive Executive*:

> We believe that scholars must concentrate on two important steps to understand the American presidency more fully. First, scholars must move from anecdotal observation to systematic description. The need to do so too often passes unrecognized in social science research. The wealth of anecdotal observation available on the presidency must be synthesized so that comparison and evaluation are as easy as possible. Systematic description reduces the information overload that precludes meaningful understanding and paves the way for the next important step: the move from systematic description to explanation (King and Ragsdale 1988).

Presidential studies are indeed moving in a direction requiring more systematic description and explanation. King and Ragsdale (and Lyn Ragsdale alone in her 1998 book titled *Vital Statistics on the Presidency*) provide data on a wide range of topics: electoral data, staffing, speeches, and position-taking on legislative issues among many others.

Quantifying presidential behaviors can of course allow the study of influence as noted in this project. However, there is also do much more that may be done. In fact, examining and testing the data developed for this project is indeed doing more. For example, this project has among other things, examined the factors that affect the "mix" of behaviors. This type of exploration, where the activity is now the dependent variable, allows inroads to be made into not only systematically describing the American presidency, but also into *explaining* it.

There is precedent for considering this notion. As noted at the beginning of this project, the ability to empirically measure and categorize congressional activity in any number of ways undeniably adds to the understanding of Congress.

Richard Fenno's (1973) work offers a case in point. In *Congressmen In Committees* he focused on explaining the activity of six committees in the

Senate of the 1960s. Fenno's premise with regard to committee decision-making is as follows:

> The members of each congressional committee have certain goals that they want to achieve through membership on a committee. . . . [E]ach committee [also] operates within a distinctive set of environmental constraints — most particularly the expectations of influential external groups. . . . In our explanatory scheme, then, member goals and environmental constraints are the independent variables; . . . and decision-making processes and decisions are dependent variables (Fenno 1973, p. xv).

In other words, by categorizing committee behaviors ("decision-making processes and decisions") Fenno is then able to develop a causal scheme accounting for the differences in behavior among congressional committees. This scheme includes both committee *goals* and environmental *constraints*.

Applying Cliometrics to Presidential Studies

The categorizations developed in this project will help presidential scholars to move in a similar direction — establishing a framework for research on the presidency. This would be a framework centered around the behavior the president. Presidential behavior would serve in part as an independent variable (the Dahl formula — see Chapter 2), and in part as a dependent variable (based on the Fenno scheme). Without such a framework, presidential scholars currently struggle with topics of the moment that seem to come and go. Examples include presidential popularity, analyses of vetoes and cabinet appointments, and legislative influence. Research is also saddled with a variety of culturally or temporally bound, "adjective" presidencies (e.g., textbook, superman, imperial, imperiled, rhetorical) that are difficult to compare at best, contradictory at worst.

This is not at all to say that these topics and studies are not worthwhile. Experience clearly shows that they most certainly are! For example, research on the variation in presidential approval ratings *can* help explain presidential behavior. James Carville was well aware of this when he scribbled "The economy, stupid!" on a board in Clinton campaign headquarters as a mantra for the campaign. The connection between economic performance and the presidency came directly from approval studies (e.g., see Edwards 1983).

Because there really are no central concepts around which scholars organize presidential literature, this research is probably not fully appreciated. The problem is that there are no *central*, specific tasks around which the presidency revolves (e.g., there are no "votes" to count, as noted in the introduction of this project). However, by creating a categorization of presidential activities (a quantitative biography), researchers can explain the presidency using the basic framework developed by Fenno which suggests that *behavior is a function of goals and constraints*, symbolically represented with a simple formula:

$$B = f(g,c)$$

where **B** represents presidential behavior, **g** represents the president's goals, and **c** represents the constraints faced by the president. This simple, understandable formulation (which is neither unusual nor unique) can go a long was toward understanding and *explaining* the presidency.

If the central question surrounding presidential studies becomes (with apologies to former Senator Howard Baker) "What did the President do and why did he do it?", the 'Fenno formula', whether accidentally or by design, becomes rather an observable feature.

The Fenno formula is really the basis for much of the analysis done in this project. Hypotheses like "Social/Ceremonial and Legislative activities should increase in election years" (see chapter 7) are clearly expressing the belief that behavior is a function of (in this instance) environmental constraints. Answering this hypothesis by noting that there is a correlation between social/ceremonial and legislative behaviors and the election cycle required using the quantitative biographical data to explore the relationship between the two variables.

The Present and Future

These types of questions, whether exploring the behavior of the president as an individual or of the White House as an institution, have been asked repeatedly. They were traditionally examined by describing the activities pursued by one or more presidents under similar situations, as done by Barber (1992) for example. More structured accounts have appeared in the literature recently as well. Examples of more structured accounts would include studies of the institutionalization of White House structures (e.g., Warshaw 1997, Hult and Walcott 1995; see chapter 9 for more on White House structures). Both the descriptive and more structured studies invariably fall somewhere into the Fenno formula. If so, all may benefit from the use of quantitative biographical data for three reasons:

Objectivity. While the type of categorization employed in this project is by no means free from subjectivity, it certainly offers more of a possibility of objectivity. Descriptive accounts are dependent upon the "eye of the beholder", which, of course, differs from beholder to beholder. This is why an adversarial method is used in trial courts. The defendant's eye, by definition, sees things differently than does the prosecution's eye (otherwise, there would be no need for a trial!). Quantitative biographical data would *start* with categorizations agreed upon by both the prosecution and defense (i.e., "intercoder reliability").

Comparison. Descriptive accounts rarely encompass more than a handful of events. The nature of descriptive writing often precludes any great number of events. On the other hand, as this project exemplifies, quantitative biographical data can include a vast number of events over long periods of time. While descriptive accounts often lead to the belief that each event is a unique occurrence, quantitative data helps find to commonalities across administrations and situations. Quantitative data can help tell whether or not presidents are unique, and, more importantly, exactly *why* they are or are not.

Confirmation. Finally, while quantitative biographical data will certainly help better explain the nature of the presidency, they are by no means a *substitute* for other types of data. As is done in this project, the quantitative data can be used to confirm existing notions of presidential behavior.

Are Quantitative Biographies useful in any other way? Yes. They are heuristic, descriptive, and explanatory.

Some Thoughts About Future Research

Given the ability to specify, record, and measure presidential activities, presidential scholars can make inroads into explaining presidential activity. To date, the factors that help explain presidential activity are identified in such a way as to be grouped into three broad areas: Personality, Context, and Policy. This final chapter briefly explores this literature and describes some of the specific factors either taken directly or inferred from that literature. Where possible, the discussion will identify specific measurement and operational approaches commonly accepted as surrogates for these factors.

Personality

A design utilizing personality variables must address three problems: First, a small "n"; second, validity; and third, reliability. In this section these three categories of problems are brought to bear in characterizing the value of various personality approaches. Most of the literature devoted to presidential behavior understandably deals with it from the psychological viewpoint (For an excellent overview of this area, see Simonton 1987: Chapter 5). In fact, most of the work on presidential behavior stems not from political science, but rather from psychology. There are many varied techniques used to assess personality.

Perhaps the most useful work to date has been done by Richard Donley and David Winter. Since their work is the most useful for present purposes, it is worth elaboration. They successfully adapted the Thematic Apperception Test for use in assessing presidential personality as a motive for behavior. This test is a widely accepted (indeed, the second most common) technique of psychological assessment. It has been refined over the course of half a century (stemming mainly from Murray 1938). The basic test "requires the individual to create imaginative stories in response to a series of [ambiguous] pictures; the content of his fantasy is then analyzed to reveal the underlying aims of his behavior" (Atkinson 1958). The "aims" are directed towards needs. The three needs used by Winter — achievement, power, and affiliation are recognized as the "three important social motives" (Atkinson 1958). Donley and Winter (1970) first applied the Thematic Apperception Test to assess imagery in presidential inaugural addresses.

These variables — achievement, power, and affiliation — are most useful in exploring the effect of personality on presidential activities. The small but fairly comprehensive and important number of categories leads to easy assessment. The categories are concise, standardized, well-defined, and widely accepted and tested — they are valid and reliable. They are based on 'first-hand' material as opposed to biographical material. Additionally, this test clearly and explicitly links personality with behavior (people act toward satisfying needs; i.e., without any needs, there is no reason to act in any manner). Winter has already scored presidents from Theodore Roosevelt through Jimmy Carter. These scores can readily serve as measurements of presidential personality.

Context

Those who developed the Thematic Apperception Test were very careful to point out that behaviors are not the result of personality exclusively. There are outside factors that shape behavior as well (see discussion of the "Fenno formula", in chapter 8, above). The environment is a less obvious, but nonetheless very important factor. Little work — of any kind except the sort of listings found in textbooks — attempts to build a comprehensive view of the presidential environment. Therefore, unlike the work on presidential personality, there exists no singular work, or set of variables, that can be singled out as convenient to use. It is still possible to amass a well-rounded set of environmental factors. Below are several such contextual factors.

Though not comprehensive, George Edwards' (1980) book, *Presidential Influence in Congress*, examines three factors important to presidential success. These can be adapted for purposes of this study:

At the end of Chapter 7, **Partisanship** is suggested as one possible area of contextual exploration once a more complete dataset is amassed. There are others:

Popularity, as Lyndon Johnson said, is "a major source of strength in gaining cooperation from Congress" (Johnson 1971). Presidential popularity has been widely examined as a topic in its own right. Among this work are suggestions and inferences (often clearly) linking popularity to behavior. For example: Neustadt (1990) notes that "the weaker [the president's] apparent popular support, the more his cause in Congress may depend on negatives at his disposal like the veto, or 'impounding;' Rivers and Rose (1985) suggest that "when public opinion is on [the president's] side he can use his influence to extract policy commitments from Congress that would not be possible in other situations;" and Ostrom and Simon (1985) suggest that "presidential attempts to influence outcomes will depend upon an ability to persuade, an ability that itself if tied to the prevailing level of public support." Canes-Wrone and de Marchi (2002) see presidential "approval as a significant resource for presidents in the legislative arena." This being the case, it is quite likely that a president armed with high approval ratings may adopt more aggressive behaviors than when his popularity is declining. Yet recent research by Bond, Fleischer, and Wood (2003) suggests that the effect of public approval on legislative success is conditioned by the levels of partisanship existing in Congress. Gallup's presidential approval polls are generally the standard measure for popularity.

Legislative Skill. This includes skill at such tasks as bargaining, threatening, timing, and extending amenities to legislators. Edwards claims that these play little or no part in success rates. However, it seems quite plausible to say that a president who is skilled at these tasks (possibly Lyndon Johnson?) would behave differently in his relations with Congress than would one who possessed fewer of these skills (possibly Jimmy Carter?). These skills may very well affect presidential activity (thus having more of an indirect than direct effect on success). Measuring Legislative Skills is somewhat problematic, although Edwards (1980) appears to have done quite nicely.

To the above variables, some others may be added to round out the picture.

Electoral Cycles. The two-year Congressional and four-year presidential cycles may very well affect a president's behavior toward that Congress. The onset of an election year may well lead the president to push more vigorously for certain types of policies. The nearing of a congressional election year may render Congress more responsive (or resistant) to certain presidential behaviors (especially on certain types of policies). Tufte (1978) found evidence of "a two-year [congressional] cycle of acceleration and deceleration in real disposable income, and a four-year presidential cycle of high unemployment early in the term followed by economic stimulation, increasing prosperity, and reduced unemployment late in the term" (p. 56-57). He concludes that these cycles are attributable to the "rhythms of political life" (p. 55). These are clear inferences of presidential behavior affected by electoral cycles. The well-documented "honeymoon" with Congress, occurring just after a presidential election is another aspect of this worth noting. The effect of these cycles on behavior surely warrant further study. The cycle can be accounted for by assigning each year to one of three categories: a presidential election year, an off-year election, or a "non-election" year. Somewhat related to this variable would be the varying state of the economy.

The Size of Proposals. Rivers and Rose (1985) suggest that proposal size will often affect its chances of success in Congress. It may very well be that presidents act differently when supporting proposals of differing size as well.

White House Structures. Another "Fenno" constraint may be the size, organization, and structure that surrounds the president. Walcott and Hult (1995) look at the development of White House structures from the Hoover administration through the Johnson administration. From this analysis, they derive seven "Governance Structures", each having different decision rules. They examine the effects of theses structures in various areas including congressional liaison.

> Presidential skill in dealing with Congress — one of the most important targets of presidential outreach — is a sine qua non of a successful presidency. During the early modern era, White House structures emerged to abet presidential efforts at legislative leadership. (Walcott and Hult 1995, p.27)

In their discussion of institutionalization in the area of legislative affairs, they note that these governing structures *are* a "constraint" on the president's "involvement in legislative affairs" (Walcott and Hult 1995, p.51). Hult (2000) later says that presidential decision-making is weakened by "reduced openness" in the executive branch that Terry Moe (1985) describes as more centralized and politicized. In other words, these governing structures do have an effect on presidential behavior in the legislative arena. They are useful as an independent variable to explore the changing nature of presidential activity.

Policy

The nature of the policy being dealt with may also affect the president's behavior. It may be useful to explore a combination of Lowi's (1979) and Wildavsky's (1966) categories. The major division being between Domestic and Foreign policy. Within the Domestic category, one can further divide things into Distributive, Redistributive, and Regulatory policies (Lowi 1979). These distinctions can be determined from simple content analyses of the proposals being considered.

Some Hypotheses for the Future

This project deals largely with overall activity. There is some additional discussion of the various classes of Legislative activities. Although the percentage of Legislative activities is rather small, the sheer number of overall observations (approximately 51,000 for the entire sample of all three presidents) bodes well for a healthy number of Legislative activities. Concluding with that in mind, here are some possibilities for further exploration based on many of the variables discussed at the beginning of this chapter.

There is also the influence of presidential activity on the success of a bill (see chapter 8 for an initial exploration of this). Here, the unit of analysis shifts to the individual bill. This requires a dataset of Congressional activity to complement the presidential activity data.

The task of gathering this data is fairly straightforward. The legislative schedule may be drawn from *Congressional Quarterly*'s (CQ) "Congressional Boxscore". It was usually found inside the front cover of each *CQ Weekly Report*. The Boxscore chronicles the path major legislation takes towards its eventual passage or demise. For each piece of legislation, it provides the dates on which committee hearings were held, and the date of passage in each house.

These two datasets move research closer to true *influence* studies, by examining which presidential activities correlate closely with the passage of legislation (for an example of what may be done along these lines, see Fett 1994).

Collier and Sullivan (1995) have already used congressional "headcount" and "conversion" data (see Sullivan 1988, 1991 for explanations on the development of this data) to raise questions about the influence of presidential approval ratings on legislative success. With a more fully developed activity dataset, one could examine the effects of *specific* types of presidential activities on headcount and conversion data.

Other topics for exploration are the effects of various contextual factors on the type of legislative behaviors chosen. For instance, in addition to looking at the effect of presidential approval ratings on success, one could examine the effect of approval the choice of activities. A hypothesis in this case might be that as popularity increases, presidents invest larger amounts of time in more Legislative activities and in more aggressive Legislative activities. Similar possibilities are the effect of policy type or economic conditions on the choice of behaviors. Still another possibility to explore would be reverse effects: e.g., to what extent do the tactics the president pursues affect popularity.

Bibliography

Adams, Sherman. (1962). *Firsthand Report.* New York: Popular Library.

Ambrose, Stephen. (1992, October). *Nixon and Watergate.* Talk delivered at Memphis State University.

Anderson, Patrick. (1968). *The President's Men.* Garden City, N.Y.: Doubleday.

Arnold, R. Douglas. (1990). *The Logic of Congressional Action.* New Haven: Yale University Press.

Atkinson, John W. (1958). *Motives in Fantasy, Action, and Society: A Method of Assessment and Study.* Princeton, N.J.: Van Nostrand.

Bond, Jon R. & Fleisher, Richard. (1990). *The President in the Legislative Arena.* Chicago: University of Chicago Press.

Bond, Jon R., Fleisher, Richard, & Wood, B. Dan. (2003). The Marginal and Time-Varying Effect of Public Approval on Presidential Success in Congress. *Journal of Politics, 65(1),* 92-110.

Barber, James D. (1985). *The Presidential Character* (3rd ed.). Englewood Cliffs, N.J.: Prentice-Hall.

Brace, Paul, & Hinckley, Barbara. (1993). Presidential Activities from Truman through Reagan: Timing and Impact. *Journal of Politics, 55(2),* 382-398.

Buchanan Patrick J. (1972, March 28). *Memorandum for the President's Files*. Memo to the president on the Republican leadership meeting. Meeting Notes Files.

Califano, Joseph A., Jr. (1991). *The Triumph and Tragedy of Lyndon Johnson*. New York: Simon & Schuster, 1991.

Canes-Wrone, Brandice, & de Marchi, Scott. (2002). Presidential Approval and Legislative Success. *Journal of Politics, 64(2)*, 491-509.

Carter, Jimmy. (1982). *Keeping the Faith: Memoirs of a President*, New York: Bantam Books.

Collier, Kenneth, & Sullivan, Terry. (1995). New Evidence Undercutting the Linkage of Approval with Presidential Support and Influence. *Journal of Politics, 57(1)*, 197-209.

Covington, Cary R., Wrighton, J. Mark, & Kinney, Rhonda. (1995). A "Presidency-Augmented" Model of Presidential Success on House Roll Call Votes. *American Journal of Political Science, 39(4)*, 1001-1024.

Cronin, Thomas E. (1974). Presidential Power Revised and Reappraised. *Western Political Quarterly, 32(4)*, 381-395.

Cronin, Thomas E. (1980). *The State of the Presidency* (2nd ed.). Boston: Little, Brown and Company.

Dahl, Robert A. (1957). The Concept of Power. *Behavioral Science, 2*, 201-215.

Dahl, Robert A. (1963). *Modern Political Analysis*. Englewood Cliffs, N.J.: Prentice-Hall.

Dahl, Robert A. (1969). *Modern Political Analysis* (3rd ed.). Englewood Cliffs, N.J.: Prentice-Hall.

Dahl, Robert A. (1984). *Modern Political Analysis* (4th ed.). Englewood Cliffs, N.J.: Prentice-Hall.

Dallek, Robert. (1998). *Flawed Giant: Lyndon Johnson and His Times*. 1961-1973, New York: Oxford University Press.

Davis, James W. (1987). *The American Presidency: A New Perspective*. New York: Harper & Row.

Donley, Robert A., & Winter, David G. (1970). Measuring the Motives of Public Officials at a Distance: An Exploratory Study of American Presidents. *Behavioral Science, 15,* 227-236.

Drew, Elizabeth. (1976). *Washington Journal: The Events of 1973-1974.* New York: Vintage Books.

Edwards, George C. III. (1980). *Presidential Influence in Congress.* San Francisco: Freeman.

Edwards, George C. III. (1989). *At the Margins: Presidential Leadership of Congress.* San Francisco: Freeman.

Edwards, George C. III, & Wayne, Stephen J. (2003). *Presidential Leadership: Politics and Policy Making* (6th ed.). Belmont, Cal.: Wadsworth/Thompson.

Eisenhower, Dwight D. (1963). *Mandate for Change: 1953-1956.* Garden City, N.Y.: Doubleday.

Fenno, Richard F., Jr. (1973). *Congressmen in Committees.* Boston: Little, Brown and Company.

Fett, Patrick J. (1994). Presidential Legislative Priorities and Legislators' Voting Decisions: An Exploratory Analysis. *Journal of Politics, 56(2),* 502-512.

Fiorina, Morris P. (1981). *Retrospective Voting in American National Elections.* New Haven, Conn.: Yale University Press.

Greenstein, Fred. (1982). *The Hidden-Hand Presidency.* New York: Basic Books.

Hamilton, Alexander. (1961). Federalist No. 68: The View of the Constitution of the President Continued in Relation to the Mode of Appointment. In Clinton Rossiter (Ed.) *The Federalist Papers: Hamilton, Madison, Jay.* New York: Mentor. (Original work published 1788).

Harsanyi, John C. (1962). Measurement of Social Power Opportunity Costs, and the Theory of Two-Person Bargaining Games. *Behavioral Science, 7,* 67-80.

Historical Materials in the Dwight D. Eisenhower Library. (1989). Abilene, Kansas: National Archives and Records Administration.

Historical Materials in the Lyndon Baines Johnson Library. (1988). Austin, Texas: Lyndon Baines Johnson Library.

House Extends Elementary Education Act Two Years. (1969). *Congressional Quarterly, 27(17),* 614-617.

Hult, Karen M. (2000). Strengthening Presidential Decision-Making Capacity. *Presidential Studies Quarterly, 30(1),* 27-46.

Johnson, Lyndon B. (1971). *The Vantage Point: Perspectives of the Presidency, 1963-1969.* New York: Holt, Rinehart, & Winston.

Jones, Charles O. (1994). *The Presidency in a Separated System.* Washington D.C.: Brookings.

Jones, Charles O. (1995). *Separate But Equal Branches: Congress and the Presidency.* Chatham, N.J.: Chatham House.

Jones, Charles O. (2000). Reinventing Leeway: The President and Agenda Certification. *Presidential Studies Quarterly, 30(1),* 6-26.

Judd, Charles M., et al. (1991). *Research Methods in Social Relations* (6th ed.). Fort Worth, Tex.: Harcourt Brace Jovanovich College Publishers.

Kearns, Doris. (1976). *Lyndon Johnson and the American Dream.* New York: Harper & Row.

Key, V.O., Jr. (1966). *The Responsible Electorate.* Cambridge, Mass.: Harvard University Press.

King, Gary, & Ragsdale, Lyn. (1988). *The Elusive Executive: Discovering Statistical Patterns in the Presidency.* Washington, D.C.: Congressional Quarterly Press.

Kingdon, John W. (1977). Models of Legislative Voting. *Journal of Politics,* *39(3),* 563-595.

Kingdon, John W. (1981). *Congressmen's Voting Decisions* (2nd ed.). New York: Harper & Row.

Koenig, Louis W. (1996). *The Chief Executive* (6th ed.). Ft. Worth, Tex.: Harcourt Brace.

Lewis, David E. & Strine, James Michael. (1996). What Time Is It? The Use of Power in Four Different Types of Presidential Time. *Journal of Politics, 58(3),* 682-706.

Light, Paul. (1983). *The President's Agenda: Domestic Policy Choice From Kennedy To Carter, With Notes On Ronald Reagan.* Baltimore: The Johns Hopkins University Press.

Lowi, Theodore, I. (1979). *The End of Liberalism* (2nd ed.). New York: W.W. Norton & Company.

March, James G. (1957). Measurement Concepts in the Theory of Influence. *Journal of Politics, 19(2),* 202-226.

Mayhew, David R. (1974). *Congress: The Electoral Connection.* New Haven: Yale University Press.

Mazlish, Bruce. (1973). *In Search of Nixon: A Psychological Inquiry.* New York: Basic Books.

Miller, Merle. (1980). *Lyndon: An Oral History.* New York: Ballantine Books.

Miller, Warren E., & Stokes, Donald E. (1963). Constituency Influence in Congress. *American Political Science Review, 57(1),* 45-56.

Minnich, L.A. (1953, January 30). *Minutes of Cabinet Meeting.* Memo to the President.

Minnich, L.A. (1956, February 28). *Notes on the Legislative Conference.*

Murray, Henry A. (1938). *Explorations in Personality.* New York: Oxford University Press.

Nagel, Jack H. (1975). *The Descriptive Analysis of Power.* New Haven: Yale University Press.

Nathan, Richard P. (1975). *The Plot That Failed: Nixon and the Administrative Presidency.* New York: John Wiley & Sons.

Neustadt, Richard E. (1960). *Presidential Power.* New York: John Wiley & Sons.

Neustadt, Richard E. (1969). The Presidency at Mid-Century. In Aaron Wildavsky (Ed.), *The Presidency.* Boston: Little, Brown and Company.

Neustadt, Richard E. (1980). *Presidential Power: The Politics of Leadership From FDR to Carter.* New York: Macmillan.

Neustadt, Richard E. (1990). *Presidential Power and the Modern Presidents.* New York: The Free Press.

Notes on the January 28, 1969 Meeting Between Nixon and Republican Congressional Leaders. (1969). President's Personal Files [PPF78].

Oppenheim, Felix E. (1961). *Dimensions of Freedom: An Analysis.* New York: St. Martin's Press.

Ostrom, Charles W., & Simon, Dennis M. (1985). Promise and Performance: A Dynamic Model of Presidential Popularity. *American Political Science Review, 30(2),* 334-358.

Pious, Richard. (1996). *The Presidency.* Boston: Allyn and Bacon.

Polsby, Nelson W. (1986). *Congress and the Presidency* (4th ed.). Englewood Cliffs, N.J.: Prentice-Hall.

Poole, Keith. (1991). Patterns of Congressional Voting. *American Journal of Political Science, 35(1),* 228-278.

Price, David E. (1985). Congressional Committees in the Policy Process. In Lawrence R. Dodd, & Bruce I. Oppenheimer (Eds), *Congress Reconsidered* (3rd ed.). Washington, D.C.: Congressional Quarterly Press.

Pritchard, Anita. (1983). Presidents do Influence Voting in the U.S. Congress: New Definitions and Measurements. *Legislative Studies Quarterly, 8(4),* 691-711.

Pritchard, Anita. (1986). An Evaluation of CQ's Presidential Support Scores: The Relationship Between Election Results and Congressional Voting Decisions. *American Journal of Political Science, 30(2),* 480-495.

Ragsdale, Lyn. (1995). Studying the Presidency: Why Presients Need Political Scientists. In Michael Nelson (Ed.), *The Presidency and the Political System* (4th ed.). Washington, D.C.: Congressional Quarterly Press.

Ragsdale, Lyn. (1998). *Vital Statistics on the Presidency.* Washington, D.C.: Congressional Quarterly Press.

Rivers, Douglas, & Rose, Nancy L. (1985). Passing the President's Program: Public Opinion and Presidential Influence in Congress. *American Journal of Political Science, 29(2),* 183-196.

Rockman, Bert A., et al. (1981). Neustadt's Presidential Power Twenty Years Later: The Test of Time. Symposium in *Presidential Studies Quarterly, 11(3),* 341-363.

Rossiter, Clinton. (1956). *The American Presidency.* New York: Harcourt, Brace and Company.

Senate Rejects Carswell Nomination to Supreme Court. (1970). *Congressional Quarterly Weekly Report, 28(15),* 943-946.

Shapley, L.S., & Shubik, Martin. (1954). A Method for Evaluating the Distribution of Power in a Committee System. *American Political Science Review, 48(3),* 787-792.

Shapiro, Robert Y., Kumar, Martha Joynt, & Jacobs, Lawrence R. (Eds). (2000). *Presidential Power: Forging the Presidency for the Twenty-First Century.* New York: Columbia University Press.

Simon, Herbert A. (1957). *Models of Man: Social and Rational; Mathematical Essays on Rational Human Behavior in a Social Setting*. New York: John Wiley and Sons.

Simonton, Dean Keith. (1987). *Why Presidents Succeed: A Political Psychology of Leadership*. New Haven: Yale University Press.

Sinclair, Barbara. (1996). Trying to Govern Positively in a Negative Era: Clinton and the 103rd Congress. In Campbell, Colin, & Rockman, Bert (Eds). *The Clinton Presidency: First Appraisals*. Chatham, N.J.: Chatham House.

Sinclair, Barbara. (1997). *Unorthodox Lawmaking: New Legislative Processes in the U.S. Congress*. Washington D.C.: Congressional Quarterly Press.

Sullivan, Terry. (1988). Headcounts, Expectations, and Presidential Coalitions in Congress. *American Journal of Political Science, 32(3)*, 567-589.

Sullivan, Terry. (1991). The Bank Account Presidency: A New Measure and Evidence on the Temporal Path of Presidential Influence. *American Journal of Political Science, 35(3)*, 686-723.

Sundquist, James. (1981). *The Decline and Resurgence of Congress*. Washington D.C.: Brookings.

Tufte, Edward R. (1978). *Political Control of the Economy*. Princeton, N.J.: Princeton University Press.

Walcott, Charles E., & Hult, Karen M. (1995). *Governing the White House: From Hoover Through LBJ*. Lawrence, Kan.: University Press of Kansas.

Warshaw, Shirley Anne. (1997). *The Domestic Presidency: Policy Making in the White House*. Boston: Allyn and Bacon.

Wayne, Stephen J. (1978). *The Legislative Presidency*. New York: Harper & Row.

Ways and Means Approves Broad Welfare Measure. (1965). *Congressional Quarterly Weekly Report, 23(13)*, 562.

White, Theodore (1975). *Breach of Faith: The Fall of Richard Nixon.* New York: Reader's Digest Press.

Wildavsky, Aaron. (1966). The Two Presidencies. *Trans-Action, 4(2),* 7-14.

Wills, Garry. (1970). *Nixon Agonistes: The Crisis of a Self-Made Man.* Boston: Houghton Mifflin Company.

About the Author

Carl Cavalli received a Ph.D. from the University of North Carolina at Chapel Hill and has taught at North Georgia College and State University since 1993. He specializes in American Institutions, with a focus on Presidential-Congressional relations. His research on presidential activity and influence has been published in the *Southeastern Political Review* and was requested by the librarian of the Executive Office of the President of the United States. He helped develop an online American Government course for the Univesity System of Georgia which won a WebCT Exemplary Course award for 2001. He also served as a political analyst for WMC-TV channel 5 in Memphis, Tennessee and has been interviewed both locally and nationally about his research and about politics.

Index

19th century, 101
20th century, 98, 101
activities, 2, 3, 6, 8, 9, 11, 12, 13,
14, 15, 19, 20, 21, 26, 27, 30, 32, 33,
42, 47, 53, 54, 55, 60, 63, 64, 65, 66,
67, 68, 69, 70, 73, 74, 76, 77, 79, 87,
88, 94, 95, 97, 101, 104, 105, 106,
109, 110
activity data, 3, 9, 54, 71, 74, 77, 79,
86, 97, 98, 99
ADA, 83, 84, 94
administration, 9, 15, 19, 20, 30, 34,
35, 36, 38, 42, 44, 45, 47, 48, 56, 60,
61, 63, 66, 75, 76, 77, 79, 80, 81, 82,
84, 85, 90, 95, 97, 98, 105, 108
AF-1, 21
Ambrose, Stephen, 53
anticipated reactions, 11
Arends, Rep. Leslie, 38
Ayres, Rep. William H., 38
Barber, James David, 27, 52, 53, 57,
59, 104
behavior, 3, 5, 6, 7, 8, 9, 11, 12, 13,
14, 29, 33, 37, 39, 42, 61, 62, 66, 69,
70, 71, 72, 73, 74, 75, 88, 89, 95, 99,

100, 102, 103, 104, 105, 106, 107,
108, 109, 110
Beschloss, Michael, 20
Bond, Jon R., 107
Buchanan, Patrick J., 40, 41, 68
Burning Tree Country Club, 60
Bush, George H.W., 15
Butterfield, Alexander, 20
Cabinet, 19, 22, 23, 32, 52, 67, 101,
103
Califano, Joseph, 34
Camp David, 21, 59
Canes-Wrone, Brandice, 107
Capitol, 1, 99
Carroll, Col. Paul, 22, 30
Carswell, Harold, 39, 42
Carter, Jimmy, 2, 15, 71, 72, 106,
107
Carville, James, 103
categorization, 3, 11, 103, 104
Cater, Douglass, 34, 37
cat-naps, 54
Chapin, Dwight, 20
Chief Legislator, 1
Civil Rights Act of 1964, 48
Clinton, Bill, 1, 77, 90, 103

Cliometrics, 102, 103
Coattail, 75
coercion, 12
Collier, Kenneth, 109
Colorado, 23, 68
committee, 5, 14, 36, 37, 38, 39, 41, 44, 67, 80, 83, 85, 97, 103, 109
Committee Chair, 82
Congress, 1, 2, 3, 6, 7, 8, 12, 13, 14, 16, 18, 20, 21, 26, 33, 34, 35, 36, 38, 39, 40, 41, 42, 53, 56, 60, 62, 63, 65, 66, 67, 68, 69, 70, 71, 72, 73, 74, 75, 76, 79, 80, 81, 82, 84, 85, 86, 87, 88, 89, 90, 91, 92, 94, 97, 99, 100, 102, 106, 107, 108
congressional, 3, 7, 8, 12, 15, 19, 20, 26, 33, 40, 42, 43, 49, 50, 51, 53, 55, 60, 65, 66, 68, 70, 71, 72, 73, 74, 79, 81, 82, 85, 87, 91, 92, 98, 99, 100, 102, 103, 107, 108, 109
Congressional Quarterly, 7, 87, 109
Congressmen In Committees, 102
Constitution, 2, 40, 62, 99
Contact, 13, 26, 56, 60, 66, 72, 73, 79, 80, 81, 82, 83, 84, 85, 86, 87, 88, 89, 90, 91, 92, 94, 97, 98, 99
content analysis, 29
Context, 99, 105, 106
Dahl, Robert, 5, 6, 7, 8, 11, 12, 26, 103
Daily Diary, 19, 20, 22, 24, 38, 39
Dallek, Robert, 55, 57, 66, 72, 91
data file, 29
database, 15, 21, 29, 30, 31, 32, 33, 63, 73, 75
dataset, 21, 29, 30, 31, 33, 37, 47, 60, 61, 70, 75, 79, 80, 85, 86, 87, 90, 91, 92, 94, 107, 109, 110
Date, 21, 30, 31, 32, 105, 106, 109
Davis, James W., 71
DDE Diary, 19, 29, 33

de Marchi, Scott, 107
Democrat, 38, 94
Democratic, 37, 42, 43, 69, 80, 83, 98
Democrats, 38, 69
diaries, 15, 19, 20, 29, 30, 32, 33, 48, 55
Diary, 19, 20, 21, 22, 24, 29, 30, 31, 32, 33, 34, 38, 39, 47
Diplomatic, 26, 54
Dirksen, Sen. Everett, 14
divided government, 75, 76, 77, 99
documents, 19, 29, 30, 32, 55
Dole, Sen. Robert, 39, 41, 42, 68
Donley, Robert A., 106
Drew, Elisabeth, 54
Duration, 21, 54
East Room, 21
economic, 5, 6, 34, 35, 36, 90, 103, 108, 110
economy, 40, 41, 103, 108
Education and Labor Committee, 38
Edwards, George, 1, 2, 3, 7, 13, 69, 72, 75, 103, 106, 107
Ehrlichman, John, 20, 31, 32
Eisenhower, Dwight D., 13, 14, 15, 16, 19, 20, 21, 22, 23, 29, 30, 32, 33, 35, 47, 48, 49, 52, 54, 55, 56, 57, 60, 62, 63, 65, 66, 67, 68, 69, 71, 72, 73, 74, 76, 77, 79, 80, 81, 82, 85, 87, 88, 89, 95, 98
elections, 12, 99, 100
Electoral, 75, 102, 107, 108
Elementary and Secondary Education Act, 38
Emphasis, 8, 12, 13, 14, 29, 42, 43, 62, 66, 81, 101
Executive, 1, 22, 23, 26, 27, 30, 32, 33, 52, 53, 54, 56, 67, 72, 73, 98, 100, 101, 102, 108
Federalist Papers, 62, 100

Fenno, Richard, 3, 102, 103, 104, 106, 108
Finance Committee, 14
Fleischer, Richard, 107
Folsom, Marion, 14
Ford, Gerald R., 38, 41, 71, 72
Foreign Policy, 7, 26, 32, 42, 54, 56, 70, 73, 109
Gallup Poll, 3, 107
game-theoretic, 5
Giaimo, Rep. Robert N., 38
Great Society, 69, 91
Green, Rep. Edith, 34, 37, 38
Greenstein, Fred I., 52, 60
Griffin, Sen. Robert, 39, 41
Haldeman, H. R., 20, 31, 32, 39
Handwriting Files, 34
Harlow, Bryce, 19, 42
Health, Education and Welfare, Department of, 13
Higher Education Bill, 37
House of Representatives, 1, 14, 19, 20, 21, 23, 27, 30, 31, 32, 33, 34, 35, 36, 37, 38, 40, 43, 44, 45, 52, 55, 59, 60, 61, 62, 65, 67, 71, 72, 79, 81, 82, 86, 91, 92, 99, 101, 104, 108, 109
Humphrey, Hubert H., 14, 22
hypotheses, 61, 100, 104, 109
hypothesis, 62, 66, 67, 68, 70, 72, 73, 75, 81, 85, 86, 87, 104, 110
inducement, 11, 12, 26, 29, 34, 37, 38, 39, 75, 76, 77
influence, 2, 5, 6, 7, 8, 11, 13, 26, 61, 73, 80, 81, 86, 90, 95, 100, 101, 102, 103, 106, 107, 109
Interstate Commerce Commission, 42
Johnson, Lyndon Baines, 14, 15, 17, 19, 20, 21, 29, 34, 37, 38, 42, 43, 47, 48, 50, 52, 53, 54, 55, 56, 57, 58, 60, 62, 63, 65, 66, 67, 68, 69, 71, 72, 74,

77, 79, 80, 81, 82, 84, 85, 87, 88, 89, 90, 91, 92, 93, 94, 95, 98, 107, 108
Jones, Charles O., 62
Kearns, Doris, 52, 54, 57, 89, 90
Kennedy, John F., 71, 72
King, Gary, 95, 102
Kissinger, Henry, 31, 32
Koenig, Louis W., 71
Landrum, Rep. Phil M., 38
Larmon, Sigur, 33
LBJ Ranch, 21
leadership, 1, 2, 3, 13, 15, 19, 33, 40, 42, 43, 44, 45, 72, 81, 82, 83, 84, 85, 91, 92, 97, 98, 99, 108
legislation, 1, 12, 33, 34, 35, 36, 39, 40, 41, 44, 66, 68, 86, 90, 92, 94, 109
legislative, 1, 2, 3, 5, 7, 8, 9, 11, 12, 13, 14, 15, 19, 20, 26, 29, 33, 34, 35, 42, 54, 61, 62, 63, 64, 65, 66, 67, 68, 70, 71, 72, 73, 74, 77, 80, 81, 85, 86, 87, 88, 89, 90, 91, 94, 95, 97, 98, 99, 100, 101, 102, 103, 104, 107, 108, 109, 110
legislator, 1, 13, 20, 65
libraries, 15, 100
Light, Paul, 71
Location, 21, 26, 30, 31, 32, 60
manipulative, 11, 12, 29, 33, 34
Medicare, 89, 91, 92, 93, 94
Medium, 26, 30, 31, 32, 33
meeting, 19, 20, 21, 22, 26, 30, 32, 33, 34, 39, 40, 41, 42, 43, 65, 68, 73, 81
Miller, Merle, 56
Mills, Rep. Wilbur, 79, 80
National Archives, 38
National Security Council, 19
National Security Meetings, 20
Negative inducement, 12, 29, 34, 37, 38, 39

Neustadt, Richard, 1, 2, 3, 5, 6, 11, 12, 62, 107

Newtonian, 5, 6, 7

Nixon, Richard M., 15, 18, 19, 20, 21, 22, 24, 29, 30, 31, 32, 38, 39, 40, 42, 47, 48, 51, 52, 53, 54, 55, 56, 57, 59, 60, 63, 66, 67, 68, 69, 71, 72, 74, 80, 82, 84, 85, 87, 88, 89, 95, 98

NOMINATE scores, 83, 84, 86

O'Brien, Lawrence, 20

Office of Management and Budget, 12

Organization, 12, 13, 29, 39, 61, 62, 66, 67, 97, 98, 108

Organizational, 39, 42, 63, 64, 65, 66, 67, 98, 100

Ostrom, Charles, 87, 88, 107

Oval office, 20, 27, 30, 32, 55, 95

partisan, 6, 7, 8, 11, 12, 14, 75, 85, 97, 99, 100

partisanship, 7, 12, 33, 65, 73, 107

Party, 6, 15, 69, 71, 75, 76, 77, 80, 82, 83, 84, 85, 86, 89, 94

Pearson, Drew, 72

Personal, 14, 19, 20, 26, 35, 38, 54, 56, 57, 62, 65, 66, 68, 71, 72, 73

Personality, 15, 95, 105, 106

Persons, Gen. Wilton, 19, 30, 31

persuade, 2, 3, 107

persuasion, 11, 12, 26, 29, 33, 34, 62, 75, 76, 77

persuasive, 3, 33, 76

phone call, 14, 19, 20, 21, 26, 32, 33, 38, 39, 55, 57, 73

Pitch, 14, 76

Pitches, 12, 13, 14, 26, 66, 76, 77

Pitching, 12, 66, 68, 69, 76, 77

policy, 1, 7, 20, 26, 32, 33, 34, 35, 36, 42, 54, 56, 68, 70, 71, 73, 105, 107, 109, 110

Poole, Keith, 83, 84

popularity, 103, 107, 110

Positive inducement, 12, 29, 34, 38, 39

power, 1, 2, 3, 5, 6, 7, 8, 9, 11, 13, 40, 62, 106

presidency, 1, 3, 48, 49, 50, 51, 52, 53, 65, 66, 69, 71, 73, 75, 98, 100, 101, 102, 103, 104, 105, 108

president, 1, 2, 3, 6, 7, 8, 12, 13, 14, 15, 19, 20, 21, 22, 23, 26, 30, 31, 32, 33, 34, 35, 36, 37, 38, 39, 40, 41, 42, 43, 47, 48, 52, 53, 61, 62, 63, 66, 67, 68, 69, 71, 72, 73, 74, 75, 76, 77, 79, 80, 82, 83, 84, 85, 86, 87, 88, 89, 90, 91, 92, 97, 98, 99, 103, 104, 107, 108, 109, 110

presidential activity, 2, 3, 6, 13, 15, 26, 37, 60, 61, 72, 75, 85, 87, 95, 97, 101, 105, 107, 109

presidential libraries, 15, 47, 100

Presidential Power, 1, 2, 3, 5, 6, 13

Presidential Studies, 102, 103, 104

presidents, 1, 3, 7, 15, 20, 29, 47, 48, 52, 54, 56, 59, 60, 61, 62, 63, 64, 65, 66, 68, 69, 70, 71, 72, 74, 75, 76, 77, 79, 80, 81, 82, 83, 84, 85, 86, 88, 89, 94, 95, 97, 98, 99, 100, 104, 105, 106, 107, 108, 109, 110

press conference, 13

Pritchard, Anita, 7, 8

proposal size, 108

Quantitative Biography, 101, 104, 105

Quie, Rep. Albert H., 38

Ragsdale, Lyn, 49, 50, 51, 86, 87, 95, 102

Ranking Member, 83, 84

rational, 11, 29, 33, 34

Reagan, Ronald, 15, 71

Reedy, George, 20

Regression, 82, 83, 84, 85, 86, 94

Republican, 13, 38, 40, 42, 53, 65, 68, 81, 83, 94

Residence, 20, 21, 26, 31

Rivers, Douglas, 7, 107, 108

Roberts, Juanita, 20

Roosevelt, Theodore, 53, 106

Rose Garden, 21

Rose, Nancy, L., 7, 107, 108

Rossiter, Clinton, 26

San Diego, 22, 32, 33

Senate, 14, 35, 38, 39, 40, 42, 43, 44, 45, 62, 67, 71, 79, 82, 91, 103

Simon, Dennis, 5, 87, 88, 107

Sinclair, Barbara, 99

Social/Ceremonial, 26, 33, 54, 70, 73, 104

SPSS, 29

Stafford, 42

strategic activity, 67, 68, 69

Sullivan, Terry, 3, 7, 8, 109

Supreme Court, 39, 42

Target, 13, 66

taxonomy, 11

Temporal, 13, 92

Thematic Apperception Test, 106

Time, 5, 8, 13, 15, 21, 30, 31, 32, 33, 34, 36, 38, 39, 40, 43, 47, 48, 52, 54, 56, 57, 59, 60, 61, 63, 64, 65, 66, 68, 69, 70, 71, 72, 73, 74, 75, 76, 79, 80, 81, 85, 90, 91, 92, 97, 98, 99, 102, 105, 110

Times, 20, 21, 48, 60, 76, 82, 91

Timing, 13, 42, 90, 107

Travel, 21, 59

Truman, Harry, 71, 72, 77

Tufte, Edward, 108

Type, 5, 7, 11, 13, 19, 26, 27, 29, 30, 31, 32, 33, 37, 54, 56, 66, 69, 73, 74, 80, 102, 104, 110

U.S. Information Agency, 33

variable, 3, 8, 21, 26, 60, 73, 76, 79, 80, 81, 82, 84, 85, 86, 94, 102, 103, 108, 109

Vice President, 14, 22, 32, 33, 67, 71, 73, 74

vote, 5, 7, 13, 14, 38, 39, 69, 72,73, 87, 88, 91, 92, 94, 103

Waggoner, 39

Washington, 27, 35, 37, 40, 41, 49, 50, 51, 60, 66, 68

Wayne, Stephen, 1, 2, 13, 57, 69, 72, 75

Ways and Means Committee, 80

White House, 1, 14, 19, 20, 21, 23, 27, 30, 31, 32, 33, 34, 35, 37, 38, 40, 52, 55, 59, 60, 61, 62, 65, 71, 72, 81, 86, 99, 101, 104, 108

White, Theodore, 60

Whitman, Anne, 19, 36

Wildavsky, Aaron, 7, 109

Winter, David G., 106

Wood, B. Dan, 107

Woods, Rosemary, 20

Year, 7, 15, 38, 40, 63, 64, 65, 67, 68, 69, 70, 71, 73, 74, 88, 89, 95, 107, 108